50 Historical Recipes Revived for Home

By: Kelly Johnson

Table of Contents

- Himalayan Yak Stew
- Amazonian Piranha Soup
- Moroccan Camel Tagine
- Mongolian Horse Milk Tea
- Australian Kangaroo Burgers
- South African Braai (Barbecue) Boerewors
- Norwegian Reindeer Meatballs
- Peruvian Guinea Pig Roast
- Vietnamese Snake Wine
- Icelandic Fermented Shark
- Kenyan Chapati Bread
- Mexican Escamoles (Ant Larvae)
- Japanese Fugu Sushi
- Brazilian Feijoada
- Canadian Maple Glazed Salmon
- New Zealand Hangi (Earth Oven Cooked)
- Jamaican Jerk Chicken
- Swiss Fondue
- Indian Spicy Bhut Jolokia Curry
- Italian Truffle Risotto
- Russian Borscht
- Korean Bibimbap
- Greek Octopus Salad
- Indonesian Rendang
- Egyptian Koshari
- French Escargot
- Thai Insect Stir-Fry
- Irish Guinness Beef Stew
- Spanish Paella
- Turkish Testi Kebab (Pottery Kebab)
- American Bison Burger
- Austrian Wiener Schnitzel
- Cambodian Amok Trey (Fish Curry)
- Danish Smørrebrød (Open-faced Sandwiches)
- Finnish Smoked Salmon Soup

- Israeli Shakshuka
- Lebanese Mezze Platter
- Malaysian Nasi Goreng
- Dutch Stroopwafels
- Nigerian Jollof Rice
- Portuguese Bacalhau à Brás
- Scottish Haggis
- Swedish Meatballs
- Thai Tom Yum Goong (Spicy Shrimp Soup)
- Tunisian Couscous
- Ukrainian Varenyky (Pierogi)
- Venezuelan Arepas
- Welsh Rarebit
- Zimbabwean Sadza (Cornmeal Porridge)
- Afghan Kabuli Pulao

Himalayan Yak Stew

Ingredients:

- 1 lb yak meat, diced into bite-sized pieces (substitute with beef if yak meat is not available)
- 2 tablespoons vegetable oil
- 1 onion, chopped
- 2 cloves garlic, minced
- 1-inch piece of ginger, grated
- 2 medium potatoes, peeled and diced
- 2 carrots, peeled and diced
- 2 tomatoes, diced
- 4 cups beef or vegetable broth
- 1 teaspoon ground cumin
- 1 teaspoon ground coriander
- 1/2 teaspoon turmeric powder
- 1/2 teaspoon paprika
- Salt and pepper to taste
- Chopped fresh cilantro for garnish

Instructions:

1. Prepare the yak meat: If using fresh yak meat, trim any excess fat and cut it into bite-sized pieces. If using frozen meat, thaw it completely before cooking.
2. Sear the meat: Heat the vegetable oil in a large pot over medium-high heat. Add the diced yak meat and cook until it is browned on all sides, about 5-7 minutes. Remove the meat from the pot and set it aside.
3. Sauté the aromatics: In the same pot, add the chopped onion and sauté until it becomes translucent, about 3-4 minutes. Add the minced garlic and grated ginger, and cook for another minute until fragrant.
4. Add the vegetables: Stir in the diced potatoes and carrots, and cook for a few minutes until they start to soften slightly.
5. Simmer the stew: Return the seared yak meat to the pot. Add the diced tomatoes, beef or vegetable broth, ground cumin, ground coriander, turmeric powder, paprika, salt, and pepper. Bring the mixture to a boil, then reduce the heat to low, cover the pot, and simmer for about 1-1.5 hours, or until the meat is tender and the vegetables are cooked through.
6. Adjust seasoning and serve: Taste the stew and adjust the seasoning with more salt and pepper if needed. Ladle the Himalayan Yak Stew into bowls and garnish

with chopped fresh cilantro. Serve hot with rice or crusty bread for a satisfying meal.

Enjoy the comforting and flavorful taste of Himalayan Yak Stew, reminiscent of the rugged landscapes and rich culinary traditions of the Himalayan region.

Amazonian Piranha Soup

Ingredients:

- 4-6 piranha fish, cleaned and descaled
- 1 onion, chopped
- 2 cloves garlic, minced
- 1 tomato, diced
- 1 bell pepper, diced
- 1 carrot, diced
- 1 celery stalk, diced
- 1 tablespoon vegetable oil
- 6 cups fish or vegetable broth
- Juice of 1-2 limes
- Salt and pepper to taste
- Fresh cilantro or parsley for garnish

Instructions:

1. Prepare the piranha fish: Rinse the piranha fish thoroughly under cold water and pat them dry with paper towels. Cut the fish into large chunks, removing any large bones.
2. Sauté aromatics: In a large soup pot, heat the vegetable oil over medium heat. Add the chopped onion and minced garlic, and sauté until they are soft and translucent.
3. Add vegetables: Stir in the diced tomato, bell pepper, carrot, and celery. Cook for a few minutes until the vegetables start to soften.
4. Add fish and broth: Add the piranha fish chunks to the pot, then pour in the fish or vegetable broth. Bring the mixture to a gentle boil, then reduce the heat to low and simmer for about 20-30 minutes, or until the fish is cooked through and tender.
5. Season and serve: Once the fish is cooked, season the soup with salt, pepper, and lime juice to taste. Adjust the seasoning according to your preference. Remove the pot from the heat.
6. Garnish and serve: Ladle the Amazonian Piranha Soup into bowls and garnish with fresh cilantro or parsley. Serve hot with crusty bread or rice for a complete meal.

Enjoy the rich and flavorful taste of Amazonian Piranha Soup, a dish that captures the essence of the vibrant and diverse ecosystem of the Amazon Rainforest.

Moroccan Camel Tagine

Ingredients:

- 1 lb camel meat, cubed (substitute with beef if camel meat is not available)
- 2 onions, finely chopped
- 3 cloves garlic, minced
- 2 carrots, peeled and diced
- 2 tomatoes, diced
- 1 bell pepper, diced
- 1 cup dried apricots, chopped
- 1/2 cup raisins
- 2 tablespoons olive oil
- 2 teaspoons ground cumin
- 2 teaspoons ground coriander
- 1 teaspoon ground cinnamon
- 1 teaspoon ground ginger
- 1/2 teaspoon ground turmeric
- Salt and pepper to taste
- Fresh cilantro or parsley for garnish
- Cooked couscous or crusty bread for serving

Instructions:

1. Prepare the camel meat: If using fresh camel meat, trim any excess fat and cut it into bite-sized cubes. If using frozen meat, thaw it completely before cooking.
2. Sauté onions and garlic: Heat the olive oil in a large tagine or heavy-bottomed pot over medium heat. Add the chopped onions and minced garlic, and sauté until they are soft and translucent.
3. Brown the meat: Add the cubed camel meat to the tagine, and cook until it is browned on all sides, about 5-7 minutes.
4. Add spices and vegetables: Stir in the ground cumin, ground coriander, ground cinnamon, ground ginger, ground turmeric, salt, and pepper. Add the diced carrots, tomatoes, bell pepper, dried apricots, and raisins to the tagine, and mix well to combine.
5. Cook the tagine: Pour enough water into the tagine to cover the ingredients, then bring the mixture to a simmer. Cover the tagine with its lid and let it cook over low heat for about 1.5 to 2 hours, or until the camel meat is tender and the flavors have melded together.

6. Adjust seasoning and serve: Taste the tagine and adjust the seasoning with more salt and pepper if needed. Garnish with fresh cilantro or parsley before serving. Serve the Moroccan Camel Tagine hot with cooked couscous or crusty bread on the side.

Enjoy the exotic flavors of Moroccan Camel Tagine, a dish that transports you to the vibrant souks and bustling streets of Morocco.

Mongolian Horse Milk Tea

Ingredients:

- 4 cups mare's milk (substitute with cow's milk or goat's milk if mare's milk is not available)
- 1 cup water
- 2 tablespoons loose black tea leaves (or 4-6 tea bags)
- 2 tablespoons butter or ghee
- Salt to taste

Instructions:

1. Prepare the tea: In a saucepan, bring the water to a boil. Add the loose black tea leaves (or tea bags) to the boiling water, and let it simmer for about 5 minutes to brew a strong tea.
2. Strain the tea: After brewing, strain the tea leaves or remove the tea bags, and discard them.
3. Heat the milk: In a separate saucepan, heat the mare's milk (or cow's milk/goat's milk) over medium heat until it is warm but not boiling. Be careful not to scald the milk.
4. Combine tea and milk: Pour the brewed tea into the warm milk, stirring gently to combine.
5. Add butter or ghee: Add the butter or ghee to the tea-milk mixture, and stir until it is melted and incorporated.
6. Season with salt: Add a pinch of salt to the tea, to taste. The salt enhances the flavor and balances the sweetness of the milk.
7. Serve: Pour the Mongolian Horse Milk Tea into cups or bowls, and serve it hot. Enjoy the creamy, comforting flavor of this traditional Mongolian beverage.

Mongolian Horse Milk Tea is often enjoyed as a warming drink during cold winters or served as a gesture of hospitality to guests. It's a unique and culturally significant beverage that offers a taste of Mongolia's nomadic heritage.

Australian Kangaroo Burgers

Ingredients:

- 1 lb ground kangaroo meat
- 1 small onion, finely chopped
- 2 cloves garlic, minced
- 1 tablespoon Worcestershire sauce
- 1 tablespoon Dijon mustard
- 1 teaspoon ground cumin
- 1 teaspoon smoked paprika
- Salt and pepper to taste
- Burger buns
- Lettuce leaves
- Tomato slices
- Red onion slices
- Pickles
- Your choice of condiments (ketchup, mustard, mayonnaise, etc.)

Instructions:

1. Prepare the kangaroo meat: In a large mixing bowl, combine the ground kangaroo meat with the chopped onion, minced garlic, Worcestershire sauce, Dijon mustard, ground cumin, smoked paprika, salt, and pepper. Use your hands to mix the ingredients together until well combined.
2. Form the burger patties: Divide the kangaroo meat mixture into equal portions, and shape each portion into a burger patty. The size of the patties can be adjusted according to your preference.
3. Cook the burgers: Heat a grill or grill pan over medium-high heat. Once hot, place the kangaroo burger patties on the grill and cook for about 4-5 minutes on each side, or until they are cooked to your desired level of doneness. Kangaroo meat is lean and cooks quickly, so be careful not to overcook it.
4. Assemble the burgers: Toast the burger buns on the grill until lightly golden. Place a lettuce leaf on the bottom half of each bun, followed by a kangaroo burger patty. Top with tomato slices, red onion slices, pickles, and your choice of condiments. Place the top half of the bun on top to complete the burger.
5. Serve: Serve the Australian Kangaroo Burgers hot, accompanied by your favorite side dishes such as fries, coleslaw, or salad.

Enjoy the unique and delicious flavor of Australian Kangaroo Burgers, a tasty alternative to traditional beef burgers that's sure to impress!

South African Braai (Barbecue) Boerewors

Ingredients:

- 1 kg (about 2.2 pounds) beef or a mixture of beef and pork, finely minced
- 1 tablespoon coriander seeds, crushed
- 1 teaspoon black pepper, freshly ground
- 1 teaspoon salt
- 1 teaspoon ground allspice
- 1 teaspoon ground nutmeg
- 1 teaspoon ground cloves
- 1 tablespoon vinegar
- Hog casings (for stuffing the sausage) - you can find these at specialty butchers or online

Instructions:

1. Prepare the casings: Soak the hog casings in cold water for about 30 minutes to soften them. Then, rinse them thoroughly to remove any salt or debris. Set aside.
2. Mix the spices: In a small bowl, combine the crushed coriander seeds, black pepper, salt, allspice, nutmeg, and cloves. Mix well to combine.
3. Mix the meat: In a large mixing bowl, combine the minced meat with the spice mixture and vinegar. Mix thoroughly, using your hands or a spoon, until the spices are evenly distributed throughout the meat.
4. Stuff the sausages: Thread the hog casings onto a sausage stuffer attachment or sausage stuffing machine, leaving a bit of overhang at the end. Stuff the meat mixture into the casings, being careful not to overfill them. Twist the sausages at regular intervals to form links.
5. Let the sausages rest: Once all the sausages are stuffed and linked, allow them to rest in the refrigerator for at least 1 hour to let the flavors meld.
6. Prepare the braai: Preheat your grill or braai to medium-high heat. If using charcoal, wait until the coals are evenly grayed out and hot.
7. Cook the boerewors: Place the sausages on the grill and cook, turning occasionally, until they are browned and cooked through, about 15-20 minutes.
8. Serve: Remove the boerewors from the grill and let them rest for a few minutes before serving. Enjoy your South African Braai Boerewors with pap, chakalaka, and other side dishes of your choice!

Feel free to adjust the spice quantities to suit your taste preferences, and don't hesitate to experiment with additional spices or flavorings to make the recipe your own!

Norwegian Reindeer Meatballs

Ingredients:

- 500g (about 1.1 pounds) ground reindeer meat (if unavailable, you can substitute with beef or venison)
- 1 small onion, finely chopped
- 1-2 cloves garlic, minced
- 1/2 cup breadcrumbs
- 1/4 cup milk
- 1 egg
- Salt and pepper to taste
- 1/2 teaspoon ground ginger
- 1/2 teaspoon ground nutmeg
- 1/2 teaspoon ground allspice
- 1/4 teaspoon ground cloves
- Butter or oil for frying

For the sauce:

- 2 tablespoons butter
- 2 tablespoons all-purpose flour
- 2 cups beef or vegetable broth
- 1/2 cup heavy cream
- Salt and pepper to taste
- Lingonberry jam or cranberry sauce (optional, for serving)

Instructions:

1. In a small bowl, combine the breadcrumbs and milk. Let them soak for a few minutes until the breadcrumbs have absorbed the milk.
2. In a large mixing bowl, combine the ground reindeer meat, chopped onion, minced garlic, soaked breadcrumbs, egg, salt, pepper, ground ginger, nutmeg, allspice, and cloves. Mix well until all ingredients are evenly incorporated.
3. Shape the mixture into small meatballs, about 1 inch in diameter, and set aside.
4. Heat a tablespoon of butter or oil in a large skillet over medium heat. Once hot, add the meatballs in batches, making sure not to overcrowd the pan. Cook the meatballs, turning occasionally, until they are browned on all sides and cooked

through, about 8-10 minutes. Remove cooked meatballs from the skillet and set aside.
5. To make the sauce, melt the butter in the same skillet over medium heat. Stir in the flour and cook for 1-2 minutes until it turns golden brown and fragrant.
6. Gradually whisk in the beef or vegetable broth, stirring constantly to prevent lumps from forming. Bring the mixture to a simmer and cook for a few minutes until the sauce thickens.
7. Stir in the heavy cream and season with salt and pepper to taste. Add the cooked meatballs back to the skillet and simmer gently in the sauce for another 5-10 minutes to heat through.
8. Serve the Norwegian reindeer meatballs hot, with lingonberry jam or cranberry sauce on the side if desired. They are traditionally served with mashed potatoes and lingonberry sauce.

Enjoy your delicious Norwegian reindeer meatballs, a comforting and hearty dish perfect for chilly evenings!

Peruvian Guinea Pig Roast

Ingredients:

- 2-4 whole guinea pigs, cleaned and dressed (available at specialty markets or from breeders)
- 4 cloves garlic, minced
- 2 tablespoons vegetable oil
- 2 tablespoons white vinegar or lime juice
- 1 tablespoon ground cumin
- 1 tablespoon dried oregano
- Salt and pepper to taste
- Water, as needed

For serving (optional):

- Salsa criolla (Peruvian onion relish)
- Aji sauce (Peruvian chili sauce)
- Boiled potatoes
- White rice
- Huacatay (Peruvian black mint) sauce

Instructions:

1. Preheat your oven to 350°F (175°C).
2. In a small bowl, mix together the minced garlic, vegetable oil, white vinegar or lime juice, ground cumin, dried oregano, salt, and pepper to create a marinade.
3. Rub the marinade all over the cleaned and dressed guinea pigs, making sure to coat them evenly. Allow the guinea pigs to marinate for at least 30 minutes to an hour, or overnight in the refrigerator for maximum flavor.
4. Place the marinated guinea pigs in a roasting pan or baking dish, along with any excess marinade. Add a splash of water to the bottom of the pan to prevent the meat from drying out during cooking.
5. Cover the roasting pan with aluminum foil and place it in the preheated oven. Roast the guinea pigs for 1.5 to 2 hours, or until the meat is tender and cooked through. You can uncover the pan during the last 30 minutes of cooking to allow the skin to crisp up, if desired.
6. Once the guinea pigs are fully cooked, remove them from the oven and let them rest for a few minutes before serving.

7. Serve the Peruvian Guinea Pig Roast hot, accompanied by boiled potatoes, white rice, salsa criolla, aji sauce, and huacatay sauce if available.

Enjoy this traditional Peruvian delicacy, rich in flavor and cultural significance!

Vietnamese Snake Wine

Ingredients:

- One or more venomous snakes (such as cobras or vipers)
- Rice wine or grain alcohol (usually a high-proof alcohol)
- Various herbs and spices (optional, for flavoring)

Instructions:

1. Selecting the snakes: Venomous snakes, such as cobras or vipers, are typically used to make snake wine. The snakes are usually caught alive and then killed before being used in the wine.
2. Preparing the snakes: Once the snakes are killed, they are typically gutted and cleaned. Some recipes may involve removing the skin, while others leave the skin intact for added flavor and appearance.
3. Placing the snakes in a container: The cleaned snakes are then placed in a large glass jar or bottle. Sometimes, the snakes are left whole, while in other cases, they may be cut into smaller pieces to fit into the container.
4. Adding the alcohol: Rice wine or grain alcohol is poured into the container, completely covering the snakes. The alcohol acts as a preservative and also helps to extract the flavors and properties of the snakes.
5. Sealing the container: The container is sealed tightly to prevent evaporation and to allow the snakes to infuse their flavors into the alcohol.
6. Aging the snake wine: The container is typically stored in a cool, dark place for several months to several years to allow the flavors to develop and mature. During this time, the alcohol absorbs the essence of the snakes and any herbs or spices that may have been added.
7. Serving the snake wine: Once the snake wine has aged to the desired level, it is ready to be served. It is typically consumed as a shot or in small glasses, often as a form of traditional medicine or as a unique cultural experience.

It's important to note that consuming snake wine involves risks, especially if the snakes used are venomous. Therefore, it's essential to ensure that the snakes are handled and prepared safely, and to exercise caution when consuming the beverage.

Icelandic Fermented Shark

Ingredients:

- Fresh Greenland shark meat (can be obtained from specialty seafood markets)
- Coarse sea salt
- Gravel or sand (for lining the fermentation pit)
- Large plastic or wooden container (for fermentation)

Instructions:

1. Procure the Shark: Obtain fresh Greenland shark meat from a reputable seafood market. Ensure that it's fresh and suitable for consumption.
2. Prepare the Meat: Rinse the shark meat thoroughly under cold water to remove any surface impurities. Cut the meat into large pieces, such as strips or chunks, depending on the size of the meat and your fermentation container.
3. Salt the Meat: Generously sprinkle coarse sea salt over the shark meat pieces. The salt helps to draw out excess moisture from the meat and aids in the fermentation process. Let the salted meat rest for a few hours to allow the salt to penetrate the flesh.
4. Create the Fermentation Pit: Dig a shallow pit in the ground or use a large plastic or wooden container. Line the bottom of the pit or container with gravel or sand to provide drainage and support for the meat.
5. Layer the Meat: Arrange the salted shark meat pieces in the fermentation pit or container. Ensure that there is space between the pieces to allow air circulation and facilitate the fermentation process.
6. Cover and Ferment: Cover the container with a lid or plastic wrap to keep out insects and other contaminants. Place a weight on top of the lid to help press the meat down and expel excess liquid. Store the container in a cool, dark place for several weeks to several months, depending on your desired level of fermentation. Check the meat periodically to monitor its progress.
7. Check for Fermentation: After the desired fermentation period, check the shark meat for signs of fermentation. It should have a strong, distinct odor and a firm texture. The meat may develop a whitish film or mold during fermentation, which is normal and can be scraped off before consumption.
8. Slice and Serve: Once the fermentation process is complete, remove the shark meat from the container and rinse it under cold water to remove excess salt and any surface impurities. Slice the fermented shark meat into small pieces or cubes, and serve it as a traditional Icelandic delicacy.

Remember that making fermented shark at home involves handling raw meat and fermentation processes, so it's important to follow proper food safety guidelines and ensure that the meat is properly fermented before consumption. Additionally, fermented shark has a strong, pungent odor and flavor that may not be appealing to everyone, so approach it with an open mind and a sense of culinary adventure!

Kenyan Chapati Bread

Ingredients:

- 2 cups all-purpose flour
- 1 teaspoon salt
- 1 tablespoon vegetable oil (plus more for cooking)
- 3/4 cup warm water (approximately)

Instructions:

1. In a large mixing bowl, combine the all-purpose flour and salt. Mix well to distribute the salt evenly throughout the flour.
2. Make a well in the center of the flour mixture and add the vegetable oil.
3. Gradually add warm water to the flour mixture, a little at a time, while mixing with your hands or a spoon. Continue adding water until a soft, pliable dough forms. You may not need to use all of the water, or you may need a little more depending on the humidity and other factors.
4. Once the dough comes together, turn it out onto a clean, floured surface. Knead the dough for about 5-7 minutes until it becomes smooth and elastic.
5. Divide the dough into equal-sized portions, depending on how large you want your chapatis to be. Roll each portion into a ball.
6. Heat a non-stick skillet or frying pan over medium heat and add a small amount of vegetable oil.
7. Take one dough ball and flatten it into a disc using your hands or a rolling pin. Roll it out into a thin circle, about 1/8 inch thick.
8. Place the rolled-out dough onto the hot skillet or frying pan. Cook for about 1-2 minutes on one side until bubbles start to form.
9. Flip the chapati over and cook for another 1-2 minutes on the other side until golden brown spots appear. Brush with a little oil if desired.
10. Remove the cooked chapati from the skillet and place it on a plate. Keep warm by covering with a clean kitchen towel while you cook the remaining chapatis.
11. Repeat the process with the remaining dough balls until all the chapatis are cooked.
12. Serve the Kenyan Chapati Bread warm with your favorite dishes, such as stews, curries, or grilled meats, or enjoy it on its own as a snack or with a dipping sauce.

Kenyan Chapati Bread is best enjoyed fresh and warm, but you can also store any leftovers in an airtight container once cooled and reheat them later for a delicious treat.

Mexican Escamoles (Ant Larvae)

Ingredients:

- 200 grams (about 7 ounces) of fresh escamoles
- 1 tablespoon vegetable oil
- 1 small onion, finely chopped
- 2 cloves garlic, minced
- 2 serrano peppers or to taste, finely chopped (optional)
- Salt to taste
- Freshly ground black pepper to taste
- Fresh cilantro, chopped (for garnish, optional)
- Lime wedges (for serving)
- Warm tortillas or crusty bread (for serving)

Instructions:

1. Prepare the Escamoles: Rinse the fresh escamoles under cold water to remove any dirt or debris. Drain well and set aside.
2. Heat the Oil: In a large skillet or frying pan, heat the vegetable oil over medium heat.
3. Sauté the Aromatics: Add the chopped onion to the skillet and sauté until softened and translucent, about 3-4 minutes. Add the minced garlic and serrano peppers (if using) and cook for another 1-2 minutes until fragrant.
4. Cook the Escamoles: Add the drained escamoles to the skillet with the sautéed aromatics. Season with salt and black pepper to taste. Cook, stirring occasionally, for about 5-7 minutes until the escamoles are heated through and lightly browned.
5. Garnish and Serve: Once cooked, remove the skillet from the heat. Taste and adjust seasoning if necessary. Garnish with freshly chopped cilantro (if using).
6. Serve: Serve the cooked escamoles hot with warm tortillas or crusty bread and lime wedges on the side. Encourage diners to squeeze some lime juice over the escamoles before enjoying.
7. Enjoy: Enjoy the escamoles as a unique and flavorful delicacy, savoring their nutty and buttery taste. They can be eaten on their own or used as a filling for tacos or quesadillas.

Note: It's essential to source escamoles from reputable sources to ensure freshness and safety. Additionally, some people may have allergies to certain types of insects, so it's essential to be mindful of dietary restrictions and preferences when serving escamoles.

Japanese Fugu Sushi

Ingredients:

- Prepared and safe fugu sashimi slices (available from specialty Japanese restaurants or markets)
- Sushi rice (cooked rice seasoned with rice vinegar, sugar, and salt)
- Nori sheets (dried seaweed sheets)
- Wasabi paste
- Soy sauce
- Pickled ginger (optional)

Instructions:

1. Prepare the Sushi Rice: Cook sushi rice according to package instructions. Once cooked, season the rice with a mixture of rice vinegar, sugar, and salt, to taste. Allow the seasoned rice to cool to room temperature.
2. Slice the Fugu: If you've obtained prepared fugu sashimi slices, skip this step. Otherwise, if you're preparing fugu at home, make sure to purchase it from a reputable source where it has been properly cleaned and prepared to remove any traces of tetrodotoxin. Slice the fugu into thin slices suitable for sushi.
3. Prepare the Nori Sheets: Cut the nori sheets into thin strips or squares, depending on your preference and the size of the sushi rolls you want to make.
4. Assemble the Sushi Rolls: Take a small handful of seasoned sushi rice and spread it evenly onto a nori sheet, leaving a border at the top edge. Place a slice of fugu sashimi in the center of the rice.
5. Roll the Sushi: Starting from the bottom edge, roll the nori sheet tightly around the rice and fugu filling, using a bamboo sushi mat or your hands to help shape the roll. Seal the edge of the nori sheet with a bit of water to secure the roll.
6. Slice the Sushi Rolls: Using a sharp knife, slice the sushi roll into individual pieces, about 1-inch thick. Wipe the knife clean between slices to ensure clean cuts.
7. Serve: Arrange the sliced Fugu Sushi on a serving platter. Serve with wasabi paste, soy sauce, and pickled ginger on the side for dipping.
8. Enjoy: Enjoy your Fugu Sushi responsibly, savoring the delicate flavor of the fugu sashimi with the seasoned sushi rice and traditional accompaniments.

It's crucial to emphasize that handling and consuming fugu should only be done by trained professionals or purchased from reputable sources where it has been properly prepared and certified safe for consumption. Improperly prepared fugu can be extremely dangerous and potentially fatal.

Brazilian Feijoada

Ingredients:

- 500g (about 1 pound) dried black beans
- 500g (about 1 pound) mixed pork and beef meats, such as pork ribs, smoked sausage (linguiça), bacon, and pork shoulder, chopped into bite-sized pieces
- 1 large onion, chopped
- 4 cloves garlic, minced
- 2 bay leaves
- Salt and pepper to taste
- Water
- Cooking oil
- Farofa (toasted cassava flour, optional, for serving)
- Orange slices (for serving)

Instructions:

1. Prepare the Black Beans: Rinse the dried black beans under cold water and remove any debris. Soak the beans in water overnight or for at least 8 hours to soften them.
2. Cook the Beans: Drain the soaked beans and transfer them to a large pot. Cover the beans with fresh water, ensuring that there is enough water to fully submerge the beans. Bring the water to a boil over high heat, then reduce the heat to low and simmer the beans, partially covered, for about 1 to 1.5 hours or until they are tender. Add more water as needed to keep the beans submerged.
3. Prepare the Meats: While the beans are cooking, heat a bit of cooking oil in a large skillet or frying pan over medium-high heat. Add the chopped meats (pork ribs, sausage, bacon, pork shoulder, etc.) and cook until browned on all sides, about 5-7 minutes. Remove the browned meats from the skillet and set aside.
4. Sauté the Aromatics: In the same skillet used to cook the meats, add a bit more oil if needed and sauté the chopped onion and minced garlic until softened and fragrant, about 3-4 minutes.
5. Combine the Ingredients: Once the beans are tender, add the browned meats, sautéed onion and garlic, bay leaves, salt, and pepper to the pot of cooked beans. Stir well to combine.
6. Simmer the Feijoada: Continue to simmer the feijoada over low heat, uncovered, for an additional 30 minutes to 1 hour, stirring occasionally, until the flavors meld

together and the stew thickens slightly. If the stew becomes too thick, you can add a bit more water to reach your desired consistency.
7. Serve: Remove the bay leaves from the feijoada before serving. Serve the feijoada hot with cooked white rice, farofa (toasted cassava flour), orange slices, and any other desired accompaniments.
8. Enjoy: Enjoy your homemade Brazilian Feijoada, savoring the rich and savory flavors of this classic Brazilian dish!

Feijoada is often enjoyed as a leisurely weekend meal with family and friends, and it's perfect for special occasions and celebrations.

Canadian Maple Glazed Salmon

Ingredients:

- 4 salmon fillets (about 6 ounces each), skin-on or skinless
- 1/4 cup pure maple syrup
- 2 tablespoons soy sauce (or tamari for a gluten-free option)
- 2 tablespoons Dijon mustard
- 2 cloves garlic, minced
- 1 tablespoon olive oil
- Salt and pepper to taste
- Fresh chopped parsley or green onions (for garnish, optional)
- Lemon wedges (for serving)

Instructions:

1. Prepare the Glaze: In a small bowl, whisk together the maple syrup, soy sauce, Dijon mustard, minced garlic, olive oil, salt, and pepper until well combined. This will be the glaze for the salmon.
2. Marinate the Salmon: Place the salmon fillets in a shallow dish or a resealable plastic bag. Pour the maple glaze over the salmon, making sure to coat each fillet evenly. Cover the dish or seal the bag, and let the salmon marinate in the refrigerator for at least 30 minutes to allow the flavors to infuse.
3. Preheat the Oven: Preheat your oven to 400°F (200°C). Line a baking sheet with parchment paper or lightly grease it to prevent the salmon from sticking.
4. Bake the Salmon: Remove the marinated salmon fillets from the refrigerator and place them on the prepared baking sheet, skin-side down if using skin-on fillets. Pour any remaining marinade over the fillets. Bake the salmon in the preheated oven for 12-15 minutes, or until the salmon is cooked through and flakes easily with a fork. The cooking time may vary depending on the thickness of the fillets.
5. Broil for Crispy Finish (Optional): If desired, you can turn on the broiler during the last 2-3 minutes of cooking to caramelize and crisp up the maple glaze on top of the salmon. Keep a close eye on the salmon to prevent burning.
6. Serve: Once the salmon is cooked to your liking, remove it from the oven and transfer it to a serving platter. Garnish with fresh chopped parsley or green onions, if desired. Serve the Canadian Maple Glazed Salmon hot with lemon wedges on the side for squeezing over the fish.

7. **Enjoy:** Enjoy your delicious maple-glazed salmon with your favorite sides, such as roasted vegetables, steamed rice, or a fresh salad. The sweet and savory flavors of the maple glaze complement the rich taste of the salmon perfectly!

This recipe is simple yet impressive, making it ideal for both weeknight dinners and special occasions.

New Zealand Hangi (Earth Oven Cooked)

Ingredients:

- Meat (such as lamb, pork, or chicken)
- Root vegetables (such as potatoes, kumara/sweet potatoes, carrots)
- Greens (such as cabbage or spinach)
- Seasonings (such as salt, pepper, and herbs)
- Water

Instructions:

1. Prepare the Hangi Pit: Start by digging a pit in the ground, typically about 1 meter (3 feet) deep and wide enough to fit all of the food you'll be cooking. Line the bottom of the pit with river stones or volcanic rocks. The rocks should be large and flat to retain heat evenly.
2. Heat the Rocks: Build a fire in the pit and allow it to burn until the rocks are extremely hot, usually for several hours. The rocks need to be heated to the point where they glow red-hot.
3. Prepare the Food: While the rocks are heating, prepare the food that will be cooked in the hangi. Season the meat and vegetables with salt, pepper, and any desired herbs or spices.
4. Assemble the Hangi Baskets: Create baskets or parcels using wire mesh or banana leaves to hold the food. Place the meat in the bottom layer, followed by the root vegetables, and then the greens on top. You can layer the food in multiple baskets if needed.
5. Lower the Food into the Pit: Carefully lower the baskets of food into the hangi pit, ensuring they are positioned evenly on top of the hot rocks.
6. Cover and Seal the Pit: Cover the food and rocks with wet sacks or cloth to create steam and seal in the heat. Then, cover the entire pit with soil to insulate it and prevent steam from escaping.
7. Cook the Hangi: Allow the food to cook in the pit for several hours, typically 2 to 4 hours depending on the quantity of food and the heat of the rocks.
8. Uncover and Serve: After the cooking time has elapsed, carefully uncover the pit and remove the baskets of food. The meat should be tender, and the vegetables cooked through.

9. Serve: Serve the hangi food hot, either by placing it on platters or serving it directly from the baskets. Enjoy the delicious flavors of the hangi, which are infused with the natural smokiness from the earth oven cooking process.

New Zealand Hangi is often enjoyed as part of special gatherings, celebrations, and cultural events, bringing people together to share in the unique and traditional cooking experience.

Jamaican Jerk Chicken

Ingredients:

- 4 bone-in, skin-on chicken thighs or drumsticks (you can also use boneless, skinless chicken breasts or thighs)
- 4 green onions, chopped
- 3 cloves garlic, minced
- 2 Scotch bonnet peppers (or habanero peppers), seeded and chopped (use gloves when handling)
- 1 small onion, chopped
- 1 tablespoon fresh thyme leaves (or 1 teaspoon dried thyme)
- 2 tablespoons soy sauce
- 2 tablespoons vegetable oil
- 1 tablespoon brown sugar
- 1 teaspoon ground allspice
- 1 teaspoon ground black pepper
- 1/2 teaspoon ground cinnamon
- 1/2 teaspoon ground nutmeg
- 1/2 teaspoon ground ginger
- 1/4 teaspoon ground cloves
- Salt to taste
- Lime wedges (for serving)

Instructions:

1. Prepare the Marinade: In a food processor or blender, combine the chopped green onions, minced garlic, chopped Scotch bonnet peppers, chopped onion, thyme leaves, soy sauce, vegetable oil, brown sugar, ground allspice, ground black pepper, ground cinnamon, ground nutmeg, ground ginger, ground cloves, and salt to taste. Blend until you have a smooth paste.
2. Marinate the Chicken: Place the chicken pieces in a large bowl or resealable plastic bag. Pour the marinade over the chicken, making sure each piece is well coated. Seal the bag or cover the bowl and refrigerate for at least 2 hours, or preferably overnight, to allow the flavors to penetrate the chicken.
3. Preheat the Grill: Preheat your grill to medium-high heat (around 375-400°F or 190-200°C).

4. Grill the Chicken: Remove the chicken from the marinade and shake off any excess. Place the chicken pieces on the preheated grill, skin side down. Grill for about 6-8 minutes per side, or until the chicken is cooked through and the skin is crispy and charred in spots. The internal temperature of the chicken should reach 165°F (75°C) for safe consumption.
5. Rest and Serve: Once cooked, remove the Jamaican Jerk Chicken from the grill and let it rest for a few minutes. Serve hot with lime wedges on the side for squeezing over the chicken.
6. Enjoy: Enjoy your Jamaican Jerk Chicken with traditional accompaniments like rice and peas, fried plantains, or a fresh salad. The spicy and aromatic flavors of the jerk seasoning will tantalize your taste buds and transport you to the Caribbean!

Feel free to adjust the level of heat in the marinade by adding more or fewer Scotch bonnet peppers to suit your taste preferences. And remember, the longer you marinate the chicken, the more flavorful it will be!

Swiss Fondue

Ingredients:

- 1 clove garlic, halved
- 1 1/2 cups dry white wine (such as Swiss Fendant, Chasselas, or Sauvignon Blanc)
- 1 tablespoon lemon juice
- 1/2 pound Emmental cheese, grated
- 1/2 pound Gruyère cheese, grated
- 1 tablespoon cornstarch
- 1 tablespoon Kirsch (cherry brandy), optional
- Freshly ground black pepper to taste
- Pinch of nutmeg (optional)
- Cubed crusty bread, vegetables (such as blanched broccoli or cauliflower florets), and/or sliced apples or pears, for dipping

Instructions:

1. Rub the Pot with Garlic: Rub the inside of a fondue pot (or a heavy-bottomed saucepan) with the cut sides of the garlic clove. This adds a subtle garlic flavor to the fondue.
2. Heat the Wine: Pour the white wine and lemon juice into the fondue pot and heat it over medium heat until it begins to simmer.
3. Add the Cheese: Gradually add the grated Emmental and Gruyère cheeses to the pot, stirring constantly in a figure-eight motion until the cheese is completely melted and the mixture is smooth.
4. Thicken the Fondue: In a small bowl, dissolve the cornstarch in the Kirsch (if using) or a little bit of wine. Stir the cornstarch mixture into the melted cheese until the fondue is thickened slightly. This helps to prevent the cheese from separating.
5. Season the Fondue: Season the fondue with freshly ground black pepper and a pinch of nutmeg, if desired. Adjust the seasoning to taste.
6. Serve: Place the fondue pot on a fondue burner or trivet at the table. Keep the fondue warm over low heat while serving, stirring occasionally to prevent it from sticking to the bottom of the pot.

7. **Dip and Enjoy:** Spear cubes of crusty bread, blanched vegetables, or sliced apples or pears with long-stemmed forks and dip them into the melted cheese. Swirl the items around in the cheese to coat them thoroughly, and then enjoy!

Swiss fondue is often accompanied by additional items for dipping, such as pickles, cured meats, or boiled potatoes. It's a fun and interactive dish that's perfect for entertaining guests or enjoying a cozy night in with loved ones.

Indian Spicy Bhut Jolokia Curry

Ingredients:

- 4-5 Bhut Jolokia peppers (Ghost Peppers), finely chopped (adjust quantity based on your heat tolerance)
- 2 large onions, finely chopped
- 4-5 cloves garlic, minced
- 1-inch piece of ginger, minced
- 2 tomatoes, finely chopped
- 1 teaspoon cumin seeds
- 1 teaspoon coriander powder
- 1/2 teaspoon turmeric powder
- 1/2 teaspoon garam masala
- 1/2 teaspoon Kashmiri red chili powder (for color, adjust based on desired heat level)
- Salt to taste
- 2 tablespoons vegetable oil
- Fresh cilantro leaves for garnish (optional)

Instructions:

1. Prepare the Bhut Jolokia Peppers: Wear gloves while handling Bhut Jolokia peppers, as they are extremely hot and can cause irritation. Remove the stems and finely chop the peppers. You can adjust the quantity of peppers based on your heat tolerance. Keep in mind that Bhut Jolokia peppers are very spicy, so use them sparingly if you're not accustomed to their heat.
2. Sauté the Aromatics: Heat vegetable oil in a large skillet or pan over medium heat. Add cumin seeds and let them splutter. Then, add the finely chopped onions, minced garlic, and minced ginger. Sauté until the onions turn translucent and the raw smell of garlic disappears, about 5-6 minutes.
3. Add the Spices: Add the coriander powder, turmeric powder, garam masala, and Kashmiri red chili powder to the skillet. Stir well to combine and cook for another 1-2 minutes until the spices are fragrant.
4. Cook the Tomatoes: Add the finely chopped tomatoes to the skillet and cook until they soften and break down, forming a thick paste.

5. Add the Bhut Jolokia Peppers: Once the tomatoes are cooked, add the finely chopped Bhut Jolokia peppers to the skillet. Stir well to combine and cook for another 2-3 minutes to infuse the flavors.
6. Simmer: Add a little water if needed to adjust the consistency of the curry. Season with salt to taste. Cover the skillet and let the curry simmer over low heat for about 10-15 minutes to allow the flavors to meld together and the Bhut Jolokia peppers to soften.
7. Garnish and Serve: Once the curry reaches your desired consistency, remove it from heat. Garnish with fresh cilantro leaves if desired. Serve the Indian Spicy Bhut Jolokia Curry hot with steamed rice or Indian bread (such as naan or roti).

Enjoy this fiery and flavorful Bhut Jolokia curry, but remember to use caution when handling and consuming the extremely hot Bhut Jolokia peppers! Adjust the quantity of peppers based on your personal preference for heat.

Italian Truffle Risotto

Ingredients:

- 1 cup Arborio rice (or other short-grain rice suitable for risotto)
- 4 cups chicken or vegetable broth
- 1/2 cup dry white wine (such as Pinot Grigio)
- 1 shallot, finely chopped
- 2 cloves garlic, minced
- 2 tablespoons unsalted butter
- 2 tablespoons olive oil
- 1/4 cup grated Parmesan cheese
- 1-2 teaspoons truffle paste or truffle oil (adjust to taste)
- Salt and freshly ground black pepper to taste
- Fresh parsley, chopped (for garnish, optional)

Instructions:

1. Prepare the Broth: In a saucepan, heat the chicken or vegetable broth over medium heat until it simmers. Keep the broth warm on the stove while you prepare the risotto.
2. Sauté the Aromatics: In a large skillet or sauté pan, heat the olive oil and butter over medium heat. Add the finely chopped shallot and minced garlic to the pan and sauté until softened and fragrant, about 2-3 minutes.
3. Toast the Rice: Add the Arborio rice to the skillet with the sautéed aromatics. Stir the rice to coat it evenly with the oil and butter. Toast the rice for 1-2 minutes until the edges become translucent.
4. Deglaze with Wine: Pour the dry white wine into the skillet with the rice. Stir continuously until the wine is absorbed by the rice, about 1-2 minutes.
5. Cook the Risotto: Begin adding the warm broth to the skillet, one ladleful at a time, stirring continuously. Allow each addition of broth to be absorbed by the rice before adding more. Continue this process for about 18-20 minutes, or until the rice is creamy and tender but still slightly al dente.
6. Add Truffle Flavor: Once the risotto reaches the desired consistency, stir in the grated Parmesan cheese and truffle paste or truffle oil. Season with salt and freshly ground black pepper to taste. Adjust the amount of truffle flavoring to suit your preference.

7. Finish and Serve: Remove the skillet from heat and let the risotto rest for a minute or two. Garnish with chopped fresh parsley, if desired. Serve the Italian Truffle Risotto hot, directly from the skillet, or transfer it to serving plates.
8. Enjoy: Enjoy this decadent and aromatic Italian Truffle Risotto as a main dish or as a side alongside grilled meats or roasted vegetables. Serve with a glass of white wine to complement the flavors of the dish.

Buon appetito!

Russian Borscht

Ingredients:

- 2-3 medium beets, peeled and grated
- 2 carrots, peeled and grated
- 1 onion, finely chopped
- 2 cloves garlic, minced
- 2 medium potatoes, peeled and diced
- 1/2 small head of cabbage, thinly sliced
- 1 can (14 oz) diced tomatoes
- 4 cups beef or vegetable broth
- 1/2 pound beef or pork, diced (optional)
- 2 tablespoons tomato paste
- 2 tablespoons red wine vinegar or lemon juice
- 1 tablespoon sugar
- Salt and pepper to taste
- Sour cream and fresh dill for garnish (optional)

Instructions:

1. Prepare the Ingredients: Peel and grate the beets and carrots. Finely chop the onion and mince the garlic. Peel and dice the potatoes. Thinly slice the cabbage.
2. Cook the Meat (if using): If using beef or pork, heat a large pot over medium-high heat. Add the diced meat and cook until browned on all sides. Remove the meat from the pot and set aside.
3. Sauté the Vegetables: In the same pot, add a little oil if needed. Add the chopped onion and minced garlic and sauté until softened and fragrant, about 3-4 minutes. Add the grated beets and carrots and cook for another 5-6 minutes, stirring occasionally.
4. Add the Broth and Tomatoes: Pour the beef or vegetable broth into the pot, along with the diced tomatoes (including the juice). Bring the mixture to a simmer.
5. Add the Potatoes and Cabbage: Add the diced potatoes and thinly sliced cabbage to the pot. Stir well to combine.
6. Simmer the Soup: Cover the pot and let the soup simmer over medium-low heat for about 20-25 minutes, or until the vegetables are tender.
7. Season the Borscht: Stir in the tomato paste, red wine vinegar or lemon juice, sugar, salt, and pepper to taste. Adjust the seasoning as needed.

8. Serve: Ladle the Russian Borscht into bowls. If using, garnish each serving with a dollop of sour cream and a sprinkle of fresh dill. Serve hot, accompanied by crusty bread or garlic bread.

Russian Borscht is a comforting and nourishing soup that's perfect for cold winter days or any time you're craving a hearty meal. It's even better when made ahead of time, as the flavors continue to develop when allowed to sit. Enjoy!

Korean Bibimbap

Ingredients:

For Bibimbap Base:

- 3 cups cooked short-grain rice (preferably Korean or sushi rice)
- 1 cup spinach, blanched and squeezed dry
- 1 cup bean sprouts, blanched
- 1 carrot, julienned and sautéed
- 1 zucchini, julienned and sautéed
- 4 shiitake mushrooms, thinly sliced and sautéed
- 1/2 cup Korean radish (mu), julienned and lightly pickled (optional)
- 1/2 cup kimchi (store-bought or homemade)
- 4 eggs
- Sesame oil
- Salt

For Bibimbap Sauce (Gochujang Sauce):

- 4 tablespoons gochujang (Korean red chili paste)
- 2 tablespoons sesame oil
- 1 tablespoon soy sauce
- 1 tablespoon honey or sugar
- 1 tablespoon rice vinegar
- 2 cloves garlic, minced
- 1 teaspoon sesame seeds

Instructions:

1. Prepare the Vegetables: Blanch spinach and bean sprouts separately in boiling water for about 1 minute, then immediately plunge them into cold water to stop the cooking process. Squeeze out excess water from the spinach and bean sprouts. Sauté carrots, zucchini, and shiitake mushrooms separately in a little sesame oil until tender. Lightly pickle Korean radish (mu) by tossing it with a little salt and letting it sit for 10-15 minutes.

2. Prepare the Eggs: Fry eggs sunny-side-up or over-easy in a skillet. Season with a pinch of salt.
3. Assemble the Bibimbap: Divide the cooked rice evenly among serving bowls. Arrange the blanched spinach, bean sprouts, sautéed carrots, zucchini, shiitake mushrooms, pickled Korean radish (if using), and kimchi in separate sections on top of the rice.
4. Make the Bibimbap Sauce: In a small bowl, whisk together the gochujang, sesame oil, soy sauce, honey or sugar, rice vinegar, minced garlic, and sesame seeds until well combined.
5. Serve: Drizzle the Bibimbap Sauce over the vegetables and rice. Top each bowl with a fried egg. Optionally, you can drizzle a little more sesame oil over the top for extra flavor.
6. Mix and Enjoy: Before eating, mix all the ingredients together thoroughly to combine the flavors. Enjoy your homemade Korean Bibimbap immediately while it's still warm!

Bibimbap is a customizable dish, so feel free to add or substitute other vegetables and proteins according to your taste preferences. It's a satisfying and delicious meal that's perfect for lunch or dinner.

Greek Octopus Salad

Ingredients:

- 1 octopus (about 2-3 pounds), cleaned and tentacles separated
- 1 onion, halved
- 2 bay leaves
- 2-3 garlic cloves, peeled
- 1 lemon, halved
- 1/4 cup extra virgin olive oil
- 2 tablespoons red wine vinegar or white wine vinegar
- 1 teaspoon dried oregano
- Salt and black pepper to taste
- 1 red onion, thinly sliced
- 1 cucumber, diced
- 2 tomatoes, diced
- 1/2 cup Kalamata olives, pitted
- 1/4 cup fresh parsley, chopped
- Crumbled feta cheese (optional, for serving)
- Lemon wedges (for serving)
- Crusty bread or pita bread (for serving)

Instructions:

1. Prepare the Octopus: Rinse the octopus under cold water and remove any debris or impurities. Place the octopus in a large pot along with the halved onion, bay leaves, garlic cloves, and lemon halves. Add enough water to cover the octopus by a few inches.
2. Cook the Octopus: Bring the pot of water to a boil over high heat. Once boiling, reduce the heat to low and simmer the octopus, partially covered, for about 45-60 minutes, or until tender. The cooking time may vary depending on the size and thickness of the octopus. To test for doneness, insert a knife or fork into the thickest part of the octopus—it should slide in easily.
3. Cool and Slice the Octopus: Once the octopus is cooked, remove it from the pot and let it cool slightly. Then, slice the octopus into bite-sized pieces. You can also leave the tentacles whole for presentation if desired.

4. Prepare the Dressing: In a small bowl, whisk together the extra virgin olive oil, red wine vinegar, dried oregano, salt, and black pepper to taste. Adjust the seasoning to your preference.
5. Assemble the Salad: In a large serving bowl, combine the sliced octopus, thinly sliced red onion, diced cucumber, diced tomatoes, Kalamata olives, and chopped fresh parsley. Drizzle the dressing over the salad and toss gently to coat everything evenly.
6. Chill and Serve: Cover the bowl with plastic wrap and refrigerate the Greek Octopus Salad for at least 1 hour to allow the flavors to meld together and the salad to chill.
7. Serve: Once chilled, give the salad a final toss and taste for seasoning. Serve the Greek Octopus Salad cold, garnished with crumbled feta cheese if desired, and lemon wedges on the side for squeezing. Serve with crusty bread or pita bread for a complete meal.

Greek Octopus Salad is perfect for summer gatherings, picnics, or as a light and refreshing appetizer. It's bursting with Mediterranean flavors and makes a delightful addition to any meal!

Indonesian Rendang

Ingredients:

- 2 lbs beef (such as chuck or round roast), cut into bite-sized pieces
- 2 cans (13.5 oz each) coconut milk
- 3-4 kaffir lime leaves (optional)
- 2 lemongrass stalks, bruised
- 3 bay leaves
- 1 turmeric leaf (optional)
- Salt to taste

For Rendang Spice Paste (Rendang Bumbu):

- 10-12 dried red chilies, seeded and soaked in hot water until soft
- 4 shallots, peeled and roughly chopped
- 4 cloves garlic, peeled and roughly chopped
- 1-inch piece of ginger, peeled and roughly chopped
- 1-inch piece of galangal or ginger, peeled and roughly chopped
- 2 stalks lemongrass, white part only, sliced
- 4 candlenuts or macadamia nuts
- 1 teaspoon ground turmeric or 1-inch piece of fresh turmeric, peeled
- 1 teaspoon ground coriander
- 1 teaspoon ground cumin
- 1/2 teaspoon ground cinnamon
- 1/2 teaspoon ground nutmeg
- 1/2 teaspoon ground cloves
- 1/2 teaspoon ground cardamom
- 1 tablespoon tamarind paste or tamarind concentrate
- 2 tablespoons brown sugar or palm sugar

Instructions:

1. Prepare the Spice Paste (Rendang Bumbu): In a food processor or blender, combine the soaked dried red chilies, shallots, garlic, ginger, galangal, lemongrass, candlenuts (or macadamia nuts), ground turmeric (or fresh turmeric), ground coriander, ground cumin, ground cinnamon, ground nutmeg,

ground cloves, ground cardamom, tamarind paste, and brown sugar. Blend until you have a smooth paste.
2. Cook the Rendang: Heat a large pot or Dutch oven over medium heat. Add the rendang spice paste to the pot and cook, stirring frequently, until fragrant and the oil starts to separate from the paste, about 5-7 minutes.
3. Add the Beef: Add the beef pieces to the pot and stir well to coat them evenly with the spice paste.
4. Add the Coconut Milk and Aromatics: Pour in the coconut milk and add the kaffir lime leaves (if using), bruised lemongrass stalks, bay leaves, and turmeric leaf (if using). Stir to combine.
5. Simmer the Rendang: Bring the mixture to a boil, then reduce the heat to low. Cover the pot and let the rendang simmer gently, stirring occasionally, for about 3-4 hours, or until the sauce thickens, the beef becomes tender, and the flavors develop. Add salt to taste.
6. Continue Cooking: As the rendang cooks, continue to simmer it uncovered, stirring occasionally, until the sauce reduces and becomes thick and rich. Be patient—the longer you cook it, the more flavorful it will become.
7. Serve: Once the rendang reaches your desired consistency and the beef is tender, remove it from heat. Discard the kaffir lime leaves, lemongrass stalks, bay leaves, and turmeric leaf. Serve the Indonesian Rendang hot with steamed rice or ketupat (compressed rice cake) for a traditional Indonesian meal.
8. Enjoy: Enjoy the rich and aromatic flavors of Indonesian Rendang, which pairs perfectly with the tender beef and creamy coconut milk sauce. It's a dish that's sure to impress!

Egyptian Koshari

Ingredients:

For the Koshari:

- 1 cup long-grain white rice
- 1 cup brown or green lentils
- 1 cup elbow macaroni or other short pasta
- 1 large onion, thinly sliced
- Vegetable oil for frying
- Salt to taste

For the Tomato Sauce:

- 2 tablespoons vegetable oil
- 1 onion, finely chopped
- 2 cloves garlic, minced
- 2 cans (14 oz each) diced tomatoes
- 1 tablespoon tomato paste
- 1 teaspoon ground cumin
- 1 teaspoon ground coriander
- 1/2 teaspoon cayenne pepper (adjust to taste)
- Salt to taste

For Serving:

- Chickpeas (canned or cooked from dried)
- White vinegar
- Garlic chili sauce or hot sauce (optional)

Instructions:

1. Prepare the Lentils: Rinse the lentils under cold water and remove any debris. Place the lentils in a saucepan and cover them with water. Bring the water to a boil, then reduce the heat to low and simmer the lentils for about 20-25 minutes, or until tender but not mushy. Drain any excess water and set aside.

2. Prepare the Rice and Pasta: Cook the rice and pasta according to package instructions separately. Once cooked, fluff the rice with a fork and set both the rice and pasta aside.
3. Fry the Onions: Heat vegetable oil in a skillet over medium heat. Add the thinly sliced onion and fry until golden brown and crispy. Remove the fried onions from the oil and place them on paper towels to drain excess oil. Sprinkle with salt while still hot.
4. Make the Tomato Sauce: In a separate saucepan, heat vegetable oil over medium heat. Add the finely chopped onion and minced garlic, and sauté until softened and fragrant. Add the diced tomatoes, tomato paste, ground cumin, ground coriander, cayenne pepper, and salt to taste. Simmer the sauce for about 15-20 minutes, or until it thickens slightly.
5. Assemble the Koshari: To serve, layer the cooked rice, lentils, and pasta in individual serving bowls or plates. Top each serving with a generous spoonful of the tomato sauce and crispy fried onions.
6. Serve with Chickpeas and Vinegar: Serve the Koshari with cooked chickpeas on the side. Drizzle white vinegar over the Koshari to taste. You can also serve garlic chili sauce or hot sauce on the side for extra heat.
7. Enjoy: Enjoy this hearty and satisfying Egyptian street food dish with a mix of flavors and textures! Mix everything together before eating to combine all the delicious elements of the Koshari.

Koshari is a versatile dish that can be customized to suit your taste preferences. Feel free to adjust the spice levels in the tomato sauce or add additional toppings such as chopped fresh herbs or pickled vegetables.

French Escargot

Ingredients:

- 24 large escargot shells
- 24 cooked escargot (canned or fresh)
- 1/2 cup unsalted butter, softened
- 3 cloves garlic, minced
- 2 tablespoons fresh parsley, finely chopped
- 1 tablespoon fresh chives, finely chopped
- 1 tablespoon fresh thyme leaves, finely chopped
- Salt and black pepper to taste
- 1 French baguette, sliced and toasted (for serving)

Instructions:

1. Prepare the Escargot Shells: If you're using canned escargot, they often come pre-packed in shells. If not, you can purchase empty escargot shells separately. Rinse the shells thoroughly under cold water and pat them dry with paper towels.
2. Prepare the Herb Butter: In a mixing bowl, combine the softened unsalted butter, minced garlic, finely chopped parsley, chives, and thyme leaves. Season the herb butter with salt and black pepper to taste. Mix well until all the ingredients are thoroughly incorporated.
3. Fill the Shells: Place a small amount of the herb butter mixture into each escargot shell, filling it about halfway.
4. Add the Escargot: Carefully place one cooked escargot into each shell on top of the herb butter.
5. Top with More Herb Butter: Spoon a generous amount of the herb butter over the top of each escargot, covering it completely.
6. Bake the Escargot: Preheat your oven to 400°F (200°C). Arrange the filled escargot shells on a baking sheet or in an escargot dish. Bake in the preheated oven for about 10-12 minutes, or until the butter is bubbling and the escargot are heated through.
7. Serve: Remove the baked escargot from the oven and serve them hot. Arrange the escargot shells on a serving platter and place toasted French baguette slices alongside for dipping into the garlic herb butter.
8. Enjoy: Enjoy the rich and indulgent flavors of French Escargot as an elegant appetizer or hors d'oeuvre. Savor the tender texture of the escargot combined

with the fragrant garlic herb butter, accompanied by crusty bread for soaking up the delicious sauce.

French Escargot is often served as part of a multi-course meal in French cuisine, typically enjoyed with a glass of white wine. It's a luxurious treat that's sure to impress your guests at any special occasion or dinner party.

Thai Insect Stir-Fry

Ingredients:

- 1 cup mixed edible insects (such as crickets, grasshoppers, or mealworms), cleaned and prepared
- 2 tablespoons vegetable oil
- 3 cloves garlic, minced
- 1 shallot, finely chopped
- 2 Thai bird's eye chilies, thinly sliced (adjust to taste)
- 1 small onion, thinly sliced
- 1 bell pepper, thinly sliced
- 1 cup mixed vegetables (such as broccoli florets, snap peas, or carrots)
- 2 tablespoons soy sauce
- 1 tablespoon oyster sauce
- 1 tablespoon fish sauce
- 1 tablespoon palm sugar or brown sugar
- Fresh cilantro leaves for garnish (optional)
- Cooked rice for serving

Instructions:

1. Prepare the Insects: If using fresh insects, clean them thoroughly by rinsing under cold water and removing any debris or unwanted parts. If using dried insects, rehydrate them according to package instructions.
2. Heat the Oil: Heat vegetable oil in a wok or large skillet over medium-high heat.
3. Sauté Aromatics: Add minced garlic, chopped shallot, and sliced Thai bird's eye chilies to the hot oil. Stir-fry for about 30 seconds, or until fragrant.
4. Add Vegetables: Add thinly sliced onion, bell pepper, and mixed vegetables to the wok. Stir-fry for 2-3 minutes, or until the vegetables are slightly softened but still crisp.
5. Stir in Insects: Add the prepared mixed insects to the wok. Stir-fry for an additional 2-3 minutes, or until the insects are heated through and slightly crispy.
6. Season the Stir-Fry: In a small bowl, mix together soy sauce, oyster sauce, fish sauce, and palm sugar (or brown sugar) until the sugar is dissolved. Pour the sauce mixture over the stir-fry and toss everything together until well combined.

7. Finish and Serve: Remove the stir-fry from heat. Taste and adjust seasoning if necessary. Garnish with fresh cilantro leaves if desired. Serve hot with cooked rice.
8. Enjoy: Enjoy your Thai Insect Stir-Fry as a unique and adventurous dish. The insects add a crunchy texture and nutty flavor to the stir-fry, while the Thai seasoning brings depth and complexity to the dish. Be adventurous and embrace the culinary diversity of Thai cuisine!

Note: Make sure to source edible insects from reputable suppliers and ensure they are properly prepared and safe for consumption. If you're unsure about trying insects, you can omit them or substitute with other protein sources such as tofu or shrimp.

Irish Guinness Beef Stew

Ingredients:

- 2 lbs beef chuck, cut into bite-sized pieces
- 2 tablespoons vegetable oil
- Salt and black pepper to taste
- 2 onions, chopped
- 4 cloves garlic, minced
- 4 carrots, peeled and chopped into chunks
- 4 celery stalks, chopped
- 2 tablespoons all-purpose flour
- 1 can (14.9 oz) Guinness stout or other stout beer
- 4 cups beef broth
- 2 tablespoons tomato paste
- 2 bay leaves
- 1 tablespoon Worcestershire sauce
- 2 teaspoons dried thyme
- 2 teaspoons dried rosemary
- 4 medium potatoes, peeled and chopped into chunks
- Chopped fresh parsley, for garnish (optional)

Instructions:

1. Preheat the Oven: Preheat your oven to 325°F (165°C).
2. Brown the Beef: Heat the vegetable oil in a large oven-safe pot or Dutch oven over medium-high heat. Season the beef pieces with salt and black pepper, then add them to the pot in batches, making sure not to overcrowd the pot. Brown the beef on all sides, then transfer to a plate and set aside.
3. Sauté the Vegetables: In the same pot, add the chopped onions, garlic, carrots, and celery. Sauté for about 5 minutes, or until the vegetables start to soften.
4. Add the Flour: Sprinkle the flour over the vegetables and stir to coat evenly. Cook for another 2 minutes to cook out the raw flour taste.
5. Deglaze the Pot: Pour in the Guinness stout, scraping the bottom of the pot with a wooden spoon to loosen any browned bits (this adds flavor to the stew).
6. Add Remaining Ingredients: Return the browned beef to the pot. Stir in the beef broth, tomato paste, bay leaves, Worcestershire sauce, dried thyme, and dried rosemary. Bring the mixture to a simmer.

7. Bake the Stew: Cover the pot with a lid and transfer it to the preheated oven. Bake for 2 hours, or until the beef is tender and the flavors have melded together.
8. Add Potatoes: Remove the pot from the oven and stir in the chopped potatoes. Return the pot to the oven and continue baking for an additional 30 minutes, or until the potatoes are tender.
9. Serve: Once the stew is done, discard the bay leaves and adjust the seasoning with salt and black pepper if needed. Serve the Irish Guinness Beef Stew hot, garnished with chopped fresh parsley if desired.

This Irish Guinness Beef Stew pairs well with crusty bread or mashed potatoes, and it's sure to warm you up from the inside out. Enjoy this hearty and flavorful dish with friends and family!

Spanish Paella

Ingredients:

- 2 tablespoons olive oil
- 1 onion, finely chopped
- 4 cloves garlic, minced
- 1 red bell pepper, diced
- 1 yellow bell pepper, diced
- 1 green bell pepper, diced
- 1 tomato, diced
- 1 cup diced chorizo sausage
- 1 cup diced chicken breast or thighs
- 1 1/2 cups Arborio rice or short-grain Spanish rice (such as Bomba rice)
- 4 cups chicken broth or seafood broth
- 1 teaspoon saffron threads (optional)
- 1 teaspoon smoked paprika
- Salt and pepper to taste
- 1 cup fresh or frozen peas
- 12 large shrimp, peeled and deveined
- 12 small clams or mussels, cleaned
- Lemon wedges for serving
- Fresh parsley, chopped, for garnish

Instructions:

1. Prepare the Ingredients: Heat the olive oil in a large paella pan or skillet over medium heat. Add the chopped onion and minced garlic, and sauté until softened and fragrant.
2. Add the Bell Peppers and Tomato: Add the diced red, yellow, and green bell peppers, along with the diced tomato, to the pan. Cook for a few minutes until the vegetables start to soften.
3. Add the Chorizo and Chicken: Stir in the diced chorizo sausage and diced chicken breast or thighs. Cook until the chicken is browned and cooked through, and the chorizo is slightly crispy.
4. Add the Rice: Sprinkle the Arborio rice or Spanish rice evenly over the ingredients in the pan. Stir well to coat the rice with the oil and flavors.

5. Pour in the Broth: Pour the chicken broth or seafood broth into the pan, along with the saffron threads (if using) and smoked paprika. Season with salt and pepper to taste. Stir gently to combine all the ingredients.
6. Simmer the Paella: Bring the broth to a simmer, then reduce the heat to low. Let the paella simmer uncovered for about 15-20 minutes, or until most of the liquid has been absorbed by the rice and the rice is almost cooked through.
7. Add the Peas and Seafood: Sprinkle the peas evenly over the paella, then arrange the peeled shrimp and cleaned clams or mussels on top of the rice. Cover the pan with a lid or aluminum foil and cook for an additional 5-10 minutes, or until the seafood is cooked through and the clams or mussels have opened.
8. Serve: Remove the lid from the pan and garnish the paella with chopped fresh parsley. Serve hot with lemon wedges on the side for squeezing over the paella.
9. Enjoy: Serve the Spanish Paella directly from the pan, allowing everyone to dig in and enjoy the delicious flavors of this iconic Spanish dish.

Spanish Paella is a versatile dish, so feel free to customize it with your favorite ingredients and adjust the seasoning to your taste. It's perfect for sharing with friends and family at gatherings or special occasions!

Turkish Testi Kebab (Pottery Kebab)

Ingredients:

- 1 lb lamb or beef cubes (can also use chicken or a combination of meats)
- 1 onion, sliced
- 2 tomatoes, sliced
- 2 green peppers, sliced
- 2 red peppers, sliced
- 4 cloves garlic, minced
- Salt and pepper to taste
- 2 tablespoons olive oil
- 1 tablespoon tomato paste
- 1 teaspoon paprika
- 1 teaspoon cumin
- 1 teaspoon dried oregano
- 1/2 cup water
- Dough or aluminum foil for sealing the pot
- Flatbread or rice for serving

Instructions:

1. Prepare the Clay Pot: Soak the clay pot (testi) in water for at least 30 minutes before using to prevent it from cracking during cooking.
2. Marinate the Meat: In a bowl, combine the meat cubes with minced garlic, olive oil, tomato paste, paprika, cumin, dried oregano, salt, and pepper. Mix well to coat the meat evenly with the marinade. Let it marinate for at least 1 hour, or overnight in the refrigerator for deeper flavor.
3. Assemble the Ingredients: Layer the sliced onions, tomatoes, and peppers in the bottom of the clay pot. Place the marinated meat cubes on top of the vegetables.
4. Add Water: Pour water over the meat and vegetables until they are just covered.
5. Seal the Pot: Seal the clay pot with dough or aluminum foil to ensure that no steam can escape during cooking. Make sure the seal is tight to prevent any leakage.
6. Cook the Kebab: Preheat your oven to 375°F (190°C). Place the sealed clay pot in the oven and bake for 1.5 to 2 hours, or until the meat is tender and cooked through. Alternatively, you can bury the sealed clay pot in hot coals for a more traditional cooking method.

7. Serve: Carefully remove the clay pot from the oven or coals. Break the seal with a knife or fork and open the pot at the table. Serve the Testi Kebab hot, straight from the pot, with flatbread or rice on the side.
8. Enjoy: Enjoy the tender and flavorful meat, along with the cooked vegetables and aromatic spices. Be cautious when opening the pot, as hot steam will escape. Dip the bread into the delicious juices and savor the authentic taste of Turkish Testi Kebab.

Turkish Testi Kebab is a unique and impressive dish that's perfect for special occasions or gatherings with friends and family. The slow cooking method in the sealed clay pot allows the flavors to meld together beautifully, resulting in a truly memorable dining experience.

American Bison Burger

Ingredients:

- 1 lb ground bison meat
- 1 tablespoon Worcestershire sauce
- 1 teaspoon garlic powder
- 1 teaspoon onion powder
- 1 teaspoon smoked paprika
- Salt and pepper to taste
- 4 burger buns
- Lettuce leaves
- Sliced tomatoes
- Sliced red onion
- Condiments of your choice (ketchup, mustard, mayonnaise, etc.)

Instructions:

1. Prepare the Bison Patty: In a large mixing bowl, combine the ground bison meat with Worcestershire sauce, garlic powder, onion powder, smoked paprika, salt, and pepper. Gently mix the ingredients together until they are evenly incorporated. Be careful not to overmix, as this can make the burgers tough.
2. Form the Patties: Divide the seasoned bison meat into four equal portions. Shape each portion into a patty about 1/2 to 3/4 inch thick. Press a slight indentation in the center of each patty with your thumb to prevent it from bulging as it cooks.
3. Preheat the Grill or Skillet: Preheat your grill or skillet over medium-high heat. If using a grill, lightly oil the grates to prevent sticking.
4. Cook the Bison Burgers: Place the bison patties on the preheated grill or skillet. Cook for about 4-5 minutes on each side, or until they reach your desired level of doneness. Bison meat is leaner than beef, so take care not to overcook it to avoid drying out the patties. The internal temperature should reach 160°F (71°C) for medium doneness.
5. Toast the Burger Buns: While the burgers are cooking, lightly toast the burger buns on the grill or in a toaster until golden brown.
6. Assemble the Bison Burgers: Place a cooked bison patty on the bottom half of each toasted bun. Top with lettuce leaves, sliced tomatoes, sliced red onion, and any condiments of your choice.

7. Serve: Place the top half of the burger buns on top of the assembled burgers. Serve the American Bison Burgers hot, alongside your favorite side dishes such as french fries, potato salad, or coleslaw.
8. Enjoy: Enjoy the delicious and lean flavor of American Bison Burgers, a healthier alternative to traditional beef burgers. Bison meat has a slightly sweeter taste and pairs well with a variety of toppings and condiments.

Feel free to customize your bison burgers with additional toppings such as cheese, bacon, avocado, or caramelized onions for extra flavor and texture.

Austrian Wiener Schnitzel

Ingredients:

- 4 veal cutlets (about 4 oz each), pounded thin
- Salt and pepper to taste
- All-purpose flour, for dredging
- 2 large eggs, beaten
- 1 cup fine dry breadcrumbs (preferably from white bread)
- Vegetable oil, for frying
- Lemon wedges, for serving
- Fresh parsley, chopped, for garnish

Instructions:

1. Prepare the Veal Cutlets: Place each veal cutlet between two sheets of plastic wrap or parchment paper. Use a meat mallet or the flat side of a heavy skillet to pound the cutlets until they are about 1/4 inch thick. Season both sides of the pounded cutlets with salt and pepper.
2. Set up Breading Station: Set up a breading station with three shallow dishes. Place flour in the first dish, beaten eggs in the second dish, and breadcrumbs in the third dish.
3. Dredge in Flour: Dredge each veal cutlet in the flour, shaking off any excess.
4. Dip in Beaten Eggs: Dip the floured cutlets into the beaten eggs, allowing any excess to drip off.
5. Coat in Breadcrumbs: Coat the cutlets in breadcrumbs, pressing gently to adhere the breadcrumbs to the surface of the veal.
6. Heat Vegetable Oil: Heat vegetable oil in a large skillet over medium-high heat. You'll need enough oil to shallow fry the cutlets, about 1/4 inch deep.
7. Fry the Wiener Schnitzel: Carefully place the breaded veal cutlets in the hot oil, making sure not to overcrowd the skillet. Fry the cutlets for about 2-3 minutes on each side, or until they are golden brown and crispy. Depending on the size of your skillet, you may need to fry the cutlets in batches.
8. Drain and Serve: Once the Wiener Schnitzel is cooked to perfection, transfer them to a plate lined with paper towels to drain any excess oil. Serve the Wiener Schnitzel hot, garnished with lemon wedges and chopped fresh parsley.
9. Enjoy: Enjoy the crispy and golden-brown Wiener Schnitzel with a squeeze of lemon juice over the top. Serve it alongside traditional sides such as potato salad, cucumber salad, or warm potato salad with bacon.

Wiener Schnitzel is a beloved Austrian dish that's simple to make yet incredibly delicious. It's perfect for a special dinner or any time you're craving a taste of Austrian cuisine!

Cambodian Amok Trey (Fish Curry)

Ingredients:

- 1 lb white fish fillets (such as tilapia or cod), cut into bite-sized pieces
- 2 tablespoons fish sauce
- 1 tablespoon palm sugar or brown sugar
- 1 tablespoon red curry paste
- 1 teaspoon turmeric powder
- 1 teaspoon shrimp paste (kapi) or fermented shrimp paste
- 1 can (14 oz) coconut milk
- 1 egg
- Kaffir lime leaves, thinly sliced (optional)
- Fresh cilantro leaves, chopped (for garnish)
- Sliced red chili (for garnish)
- Banana leaves or aluminum foil (for wrapping)
- Steamed jasmine rice (for serving)

Instructions:

1. Prepare the Fish: In a bowl, combine the fish sauce, palm sugar, red curry paste, turmeric powder, and shrimp paste. Mix well to form a smooth paste.
2. Marinate the Fish: Add the fish fillets to the bowl with the marinade and toss to coat the fish evenly. Let the fish marinate for at least 30 minutes to allow the flavors to penetrate.
3. Prepare the Coconut Mixture: In a separate bowl, whisk together the coconut milk and egg until well combined. This will be the base of the curry.
4. Assemble the Amok Trey: Place a few spoonfuls of the coconut mixture into each banana leaf or aluminum foil packet. Add a portion of the marinated fish on top of the coconut mixture. Spoon a little more coconut mixture over the fish to cover it.
5. Wrap and Steam: Fold the banana leaves or aluminum foil to form packets, ensuring that they are sealed tightly to prevent any steam from escaping. Place the packets in a steamer or on a rack over boiling water and steam for about 20-25 minutes, or until the fish is cooked through and the curry is set.
6. Garnish and Serve: Once the Amok Trey is cooked, carefully open the packets. Garnish with thinly sliced kaffir lime leaves, chopped cilantro leaves, and sliced red chili.

7. Serve: Serve the Cambodian Amok Trey hot with steamed jasmine rice on the side.
8. Enjoy: Enjoy the rich and aromatic flavors of Cambodian Amok Trey, a delicious and comforting dish that's perfect for sharing with friends and family.

This traditional Cambodian dish is often served as part of a multi-course meal or during special occasions and celebrations. The creamy coconut curry pairs beautifully with the tender fish, creating a flavorful and satisfying dish.

Danish Smørrebrød (Open-faced Sandwiches)

Ingredients:

- Dense rye bread or pumpernickel bread, sliced
- Butter or mayonnaise (optional)
- Various toppings such as sliced meats (e.g., roast beef, smoked salmon, ham), cheeses (e.g., Havarti, Danish blue cheese), pickled vegetables (e.g., cucumbers, red onions), boiled eggs, herring, shrimp, pâté, liverwurst, smoked mackerel, or smoked eel
- Garnishes such as fresh herbs (e.g., dill, parsley), radishes, lemon wedges, capers, or edible flowers

Instructions:

1. Prepare the Bread: Start by slicing the dense rye bread or pumpernickel bread into thick slices. You can lightly toast the bread if desired.
2. Spread Butter or Mayonnaise (Optional): If using, spread a thin layer of butter or mayonnaise on each slice of bread. This adds richness and helps the toppings adhere to the bread.
3. Add the Toppings: Arrange your chosen toppings on the bread slices. Get creative and mix and match flavors and textures to create a variety of Smørrebrød. Here are some classic combinations to try:
    - Roast beef with remoulade (a Danish condiment similar to tartar sauce) and crispy onions
    - Smoked salmon with cream cheese, sliced cucumber, and fresh dill
    - Liver pâté with pickled red onions and cornichons
    - Pickled herring with sliced boiled eggs, red onion rings, and capers
    - Shrimp with mayonnaise, lemon wedges, and chopped chives
    - Danish blue cheese with sliced pear, honey, and toasted walnuts
4. Garnish: Add garnishes to enhance the appearance and flavor of the Smørrebrød. Sprinkle fresh herbs over the top, add slices of radish for crunch, or garnish with lemon wedges, capers, or edible flowers for a decorative touch.
5. Serve: Arrange the prepared Danish Smørrebrød on a platter and serve them as an appetizer, light meal, or part of a Danish-style brunch or lunch spread.
6. Enjoy: Enjoy the delightful flavors and textures of Danish Smørrebrød, a quintessential part of Danish culinary culture. Pair them with a refreshing Danish beer or aquavit for an authentic dining experience.

Danish Smørrebrød are highly customizable, so feel free to experiment with different toppings and flavor combinations to suit your taste preferences. They're perfect for entertaining guests or enjoying a simple yet elegant meal at home.

Finnish Smoked Salmon Soup

Ingredients:

- 1 lb (about 450g) smoked salmon fillets, skin removed, cut into bite-sized pieces
- 4 cups fish or vegetable broth
- 1 onion, finely chopped
- 2 carrots, diced
- 2 celery stalks, diced
- 2 medium potatoes, peeled and diced
- 1 bay leaf
- 1 teaspoon whole black peppercorns
- 1 cup heavy cream
- 2 tablespoons butter
- 2 tablespoons all-purpose flour
- 1/4 cup chopped fresh dill
- Salt and pepper to taste
- Lemon wedges, for serving
- Crusty bread or Finnish rye bread, for serving

Instructions:

1. Prepare the Vegetables: In a large soup pot, melt the butter over medium heat. Add the chopped onion, diced carrots, and diced celery. Sauté for 5-7 minutes, or until the vegetables are softened.
2. Add Potatoes and Broth: Add the diced potatoes, fish or vegetable broth, bay leaf, and whole black peppercorns to the pot. Bring the mixture to a boil, then reduce the heat to low and simmer for about 15-20 minutes, or until the potatoes are tender.
3. Make the Roux: In a separate small saucepan, melt the remaining butter over medium heat. Stir in the flour to form a paste. Cook the roux, stirring constantly, for 1-2 minutes to remove the raw flour taste.
4. Thicken the Soup: Gradually whisk in the heavy cream, stirring constantly to prevent lumps from forming. Cook the mixture for another 2-3 minutes, or until it thickens slightly.
5. Combine and Simmer: Pour the cream mixture into the soup pot with the cooked vegetables and broth. Stir to combine. Add the smoked salmon pieces and chopped fresh dill to the pot. Season with salt and pepper to taste.

6. Simmer and Serve: Simmer the soup gently for another 5 minutes to allow the flavors to meld together. Taste and adjust seasoning if needed.
7. Serve: Ladle the Finnish Smoked Salmon Soup into bowls. Serve hot with lemon wedges on the side for squeezing over the soup. Enjoy with crusty bread or Finnish rye bread for a complete meal.
8. Enjoy: Enjoy the creamy and flavorful Finnish Smoked Salmon Soup, a comforting dish perfect for chilly days or as a starter for a special meal.

This soup is a beloved classic in Finnish cuisine, often enjoyed during the colder months of the year. The combination of smoked salmon, creamy broth, and fragrant dill makes it a delightful and satisfying dish for any occasion.

Israeli Shakshuka

Ingredients:

- 2 tablespoons olive oil
- 1 onion, finely chopped
- 1 bell pepper (red, yellow, or orange), diced
- 2 cloves garlic, minced
- 1 teaspoon ground cumin
- 1 teaspoon paprika
- 1/4 teaspoon cayenne pepper (optional, for extra heat)
- 1 can (14 oz) diced tomatoes
- Salt and black pepper to taste
- 4-6 large eggs
- Fresh parsley or cilantro, chopped, for garnish
- Crumbled feta cheese or goat cheese (optional, for serving)
- Crusty bread or pita, for serving

Instructions:

1. Sauté Vegetables: Heat the olive oil in a large skillet or cast-iron pan over medium heat. Add the chopped onion and diced bell pepper. Sauté for 5-7 minutes, or until the vegetables are softened.
2. Add Garlic and Spices: Stir in the minced garlic, ground cumin, paprika, and cayenne pepper (if using). Cook for another minute, or until the spices are fragrant.
3. Add Tomatoes: Pour the diced tomatoes (with their juices) into the skillet. Stir to combine with the sautéed vegetables and spices. Season the mixture with salt and black pepper to taste.
4. Simmer Sauce: Reduce the heat to medium-low and let the sauce simmer for about 10-15 minutes, or until it thickens slightly. If the sauce becomes too thick, you can add a splash of water to thin it out.
5. Create Wells for Eggs: Using a spoon, create small wells in the sauce for each egg. Crack each egg into a separate well, taking care not to break the yolks.
6. Poach Eggs: Cover the skillet with a lid and let the eggs cook in the sauce for about 5-7 minutes, or until the egg whites are set but the yolks are still runny. Keep an eye on the eggs to prevent overcooking.

7. Garnish and Serve: Once the eggs are cooked to your liking, remove the skillet from the heat. Sprinkle chopped fresh parsley or cilantro over the top for garnish. Optionally, crumble feta cheese or goat cheese over the shakshuka for added flavor.
8. Serve: Serve the Israeli Shakshuka hot directly from the skillet. Scoop the eggs and sauce onto plates and enjoy with crusty bread or pita for dipping.

Israeli Shakshuka is a flavorful and satisfying dish that's perfect for breakfast, brunch, or even a quick and easy dinner. It's versatile, comforting, and packed with protein and nutrients.

Lebanese Mezze Platter
1. Hummus: A creamy dip made from chickpeas, tahini (sesame seed paste), lemon juice, garlic, and olive oil.
2. Baba Ganoush: A smoky eggplant dip made with roasted eggplant, tahini, garlic, lemon juice, and olive oil.
3. Tabbouleh: A refreshing salad made with finely chopped parsley, bulgur wheat, tomatoes, onions, mint, and dressed with lemon juice and olive oil.
4. Fattoush: A colorful salad made with mixed greens, cucumber, tomato, radish, onion, and crispy pieces of toasted pita bread, dressed with sumac and a tangy vinaigrette.
5. Labneh: Thick and creamy strained yogurt, often served drizzled with olive oil and sprinkled with herbs or spices.
6. Muhammara: A spicy red pepper and walnut dip, flavored with garlic, lemon juice, and pomegranate molasses.
7. Falafel: Deep-fried chickpea or fava bean patties, served with tahini sauce or garlic yogurt sauce.
8. Kibbeh: Deep-fried or baked bulgur wheat and ground meat (usually lamb or beef) patties, stuffed with a savory filling of spiced meat, onions, and pine nuts.
9. Stuffed Grape Leaves (Warak Enab): Grape leaves stuffed with a mixture of rice, herbs, and sometimes ground meat, cooked with lemon juice and olive oil.
10. Olives and Pickles: Assorted olives, pickled vegetables such as cucumbers, turnips, and carrots, often flavored with garlic, herbs, and spices.
11. Cheese: Varieties of Lebanese cheeses such as halloumi, akkawi, or labneh balls rolled in za'atar.
12. Flatbread: Warm pita bread or Lebanese flatbread, served for dipping and scooping up the mezze.

To assemble a Lebanese mezze platter, arrange the dishes attractively on a large serving platter or board, leaving space for guests to help themselves. Serve with extra pita bread or flatbread on the side. Don't forget to garnish with fresh herbs, lemon wedges, and a drizzle of olive oil for an extra touch of flavor and presentation. Enjoy the vibrant flavors and textures of this delicious spread with friends and family!

Malaysian Nasi Goreng

Ingredients:

- 3 cups cooked long-grain white rice, preferably cooled or day-old
- 2 tablespoons vegetable oil
- 2 cloves garlic, minced
- 1 small onion, finely chopped
- 2 eggs, lightly beaten
- 1 cup cooked chicken, shrimp, or tofu, diced (optional)
- 1 cup mixed vegetables (such as peas, carrots, and bell peppers), diced
- 2 tablespoons soy sauce
- 1 tablespoon oyster sauce
- 1 tablespoon kecap manis (sweet soy sauce)
- 1 teaspoon sambal oelek or chili paste (adjust to taste)
- Salt and pepper to taste
- Sliced cucumbers, tomatoes, and lime wedges for garnish
- Fried shallots or chopped scallions for garnish

Instructions:

1. Prepare the Ingredients: If you haven't already, cook the rice according to package instructions and allow it to cool. Prepare any meats, seafood, or tofu you plan to use, and dice the vegetables.
2. Heat the Oil: Heat the vegetable oil in a large skillet or wok over medium-high heat.

3. Sauté Aromatics: Add the minced garlic and chopped onion to the skillet. Sauté for 1-2 minutes until fragrant and the onions are translucent.
4. Cook the Eggs: Push the garlic and onion mixture to one side of the skillet. Pour the beaten eggs into the empty side of the skillet. Allow them to cook undisturbed for a minute or so, then scramble them until cooked through. Mix the scrambled eggs with the garlic and onion mixture.
5. Add Protein and Vegetables: Add the cooked chicken, shrimp, or tofu (if using) to the skillet, along with the diced mixed vegetables. Stir-fry for a few minutes until heated through and the vegetables are tender-crisp.
6. Add Rice: Add the cooked rice to the skillet, breaking up any clumps with a spatula. Stir-fry everything together, ensuring the rice is well-coated with the other ingredients.
7. Season the Rice: Drizzle the soy sauce, oyster sauce, and kecap manis (sweet soy sauce) over the rice. Add the sambal oelek or chili paste for a spicy kick. Season with salt and pepper to taste. Continue stir-frying until everything is evenly combined and heated through.
8. Garnish and Serve: Transfer the Nasi Goreng to serving plates or bowls. Garnish with sliced cucumbers, tomatoes, lime wedges, and fried shallots or chopped scallions.
9. Enjoy: Serve the Malaysian Nasi Goreng hot, accompanied by additional sambal oelek or chili paste for those who like it spicier. Enjoy this flavorful and satisfying dish as a main course or as part of a larger Malaysian feast!

Feel free to customize this recipe with your favorite ingredients and adjust the seasonings to suit your taste preferences. Nasi Goreng is versatile and can be made with various proteins, vegetables, and spice levels, making it a delicious and flexible dish for any occasion.

Dutch Stroopwafels

Ingredients:

For the Dough:

- 2 cups (250g) all-purpose flour
- 1/2 cup (100g) granulated sugar
- 1/2 cup (115g) unsalted butter, softened
- 1 large egg
- 1 teaspoon active dry yeast
- 1/4 cup (60ml) warm milk
- 1/2 teaspoon ground cinnamon
- Pinch of salt

For the Caramel Filling:

- 1 cup (200g) brown sugar
- 1/2 cup (115g) unsalted butter
- 1/4 cup (60ml) light corn syrup
- 1/4 cup (60ml) heavy cream
- 1 teaspoon vanilla extract
- Pinch of salt

Instructions:

1. Activate the Yeast: In a small bowl, dissolve the active dry yeast in warm milk. Let it sit for about 5-10 minutes, or until frothy.
2. Make the Dough: In a large mixing bowl, cream together the softened butter and granulated sugar until light and fluffy. Add the egg and mix until well combined. Gradually add the flour, ground cinnamon, and a pinch of salt, mixing until a smooth dough forms. Finally, add the activated yeast mixture and knead until the dough is smooth and elastic. Cover the bowl with plastic wrap and let the dough rest in a warm place for about 1 hour, or until it doubles in size.
3. Prepare the Caramel Filling: While the dough is rising, make the caramel filling. In a saucepan, combine the brown sugar, unsalted butter, light corn syrup, heavy cream, vanilla extract, and a pinch of salt. Cook over medium heat, stirring

constantly, until the mixture comes to a gentle boil. Reduce the heat to low and let the caramel simmer for about 5 minutes, stirring occasionally, until it thickens slightly. Remove from heat and let it cool slightly.
4. Preheat the Waffle Iron: Preheat a stroopwafel iron or a regular waffle iron according to manufacturer's instructions.
5. Form the Stroopwafels: Divide the risen dough into small balls, about 1 tablespoon each. Place a ball of dough onto the preheated waffle iron and cook until golden brown and crispy. Remove the waffle from the iron and immediately cut it in half horizontally to form two thin waffle cookies. While the waffle is still warm, spread a thin layer of caramel filling on one half and top it with the other half to create a sandwich. Press gently to adhere the cookies together. Repeat with the remaining dough and caramel filling.
6. Serve and Enjoy: Serve the Dutch Stroopwafels warm with a cup of coffee or tea. Enjoy the delightful combination of crispy waffle cookies and gooey caramel filling!

Stroopwafels are best enjoyed fresh, but they can be stored in an airtight container for a few days. To reheat, simply warm them in a low oven for a few minutes before serving. These homemade stroopwafels make a wonderful treat for any occasion and are sure to impress your family and friends!

Nigerian Jollof Rice

Ingredients:

- 2 cups long-grain parboiled rice
- 3-4 ripe tomatoes, blended into a puree
- 1 large onion, finely chopped
- 1 red bell pepper, finely chopped
- 1 green bell pepper, finely chopped
- 2-3 Scotch bonnet peppers (adjust to taste), finely chopped
- 3 cloves garlic, minced
- 1 inch ginger, grated
- 2 tablespoons tomato paste
- 1/4 cup vegetable oil
- 2 cups chicken or vegetable broth
- 1 teaspoon ground cumin
- 1 teaspoon ground coriander
- 1 teaspoon thyme
- 1 teaspoon curry powder
- 1 teaspoon paprika
- Salt and pepper to taste
- 1 cup mixed vegetables (such as peas, carrots, and green beans), diced (optional)
- Cooked chicken, beef, or fish for serving (optional)

Instructions:

1. Prepare the Ingredients: Rinse the parboiled rice under cold water until the water runs clear. Drain and set aside. Blend the tomatoes into a smooth puree and chop the onions, bell peppers, and Scotch bonnet peppers. Mince the garlic and grate the ginger.
2. Sauté Aromatics: Heat the vegetable oil in a large pot or Dutch oven over medium heat. Add the chopped onions and sauté until translucent, about 3-4 minutes. Stir in the minced garlic and grated ginger and cook for another minute until fragrant.
3. Add Tomato Paste and Puree: Add the tomato paste to the pot and cook, stirring constantly, for 2-3 minutes to caramelize the paste slightly. Pour in the blended tomato puree and cook, stirring occasionally, for about 10-15 minutes until the puree thickens and the raw taste of the tomatoes is gone.

4. Season the Sauce: Add the chopped bell peppers and Scotch bonnet peppers to the pot, along with the ground cumin, ground coriander, thyme, curry powder, paprika, salt, and pepper. Stir to combine and let the sauce simmer for another 5-10 minutes to allow the flavors to meld together.
5. Cook the Rice: Add the parboiled rice to the pot, stirring until it is well coated with the tomato sauce. Pour in the chicken or vegetable broth, ensuring that the rice is completely submerged in liquid. If using mixed vegetables, add them to the pot at this stage. Bring the mixture to a gentle boil, then reduce the heat to low. Cover the pot with a tight-fitting lid and let the rice simmer for about 20-25 minutes, or until the rice is cooked through and the liquid is absorbed. If the rice is still too firm, add a little more broth or water and continue cooking until done.
6. Fluff and Serve: Once the rice is cooked, remove the pot from the heat and let it sit, covered, for a few minutes. Use a fork to fluff the rice gently, mixing in any vegetables if added. Serve the Nigerian Jollof Rice hot, accompanied by cooked chicken, beef, or fish if desired.
7. Enjoy: Enjoy the delicious and flavorful Nigerian Jollof Rice, a classic West African dish that's perfect for sharing with family and friends!

Nigerian Jollof Rice is often served at celebrations, gatherings, and special occasions, and it's sure to be a hit with its vibrant colors and bold flavors. Feel free to adjust the level of spiciness to suit your taste preferences, and customize the dish with your favorite protein and vegetables.

Portuguese Bacalhau à Brás

Ingredients:

- 1 lb (450g) salted cod (bacalhau), soaked and desalted
- 4 large potatoes, peeled and cut into matchsticks or thinly sliced
- 1 large onion, thinly sliced
- 4 cloves garlic, minced
- 4 eggs, lightly beaten
- 1/4 cup (60ml) olive oil
- Salt and pepper to taste
- Fresh parsley, chopped, for garnish
- Black olives, for garnish (optional)

Instructions:

1. Prepare the Salted Cod: Rinse the salted cod under cold water to remove excess salt. Place it in a bowl and cover it with cold water. Let it soak in the refrigerator for at least 24 hours, changing the water 2-3 times. Once desalted, drain the cod and pat it dry with paper towels. Remove any bones and skin, then shred the cod into small pieces.
2. Cook the Potatoes: Heat the olive oil in a large skillet over medium heat. Add the sliced potatoes and fry until golden brown and crispy, about 8-10 minutes. Remove the potatoes from the skillet and drain them on paper towels to remove excess oil.
3. Sauté the Onions and Garlic: In the same skillet, add the thinly sliced onion and minced garlic. Sauté until the onions are soft and translucent, about 5-7 minutes.
4. Add the Salted Cod: Add the shredded salted cod to the skillet with the onions and garlic. Cook for another 3-4 minutes, stirring occasionally, until the cod is heated through.
5. Combine with Potatoes: Add the fried potatoes to the skillet with the cod mixture. Stir to combine, making sure the potatoes are evenly distributed.
6. Add the Eggs: Pour the lightly beaten eggs over the mixture in the skillet. Stir gently to combine, allowing the eggs to cook and form a creamy coating around the cod and potatoes. Cook for 2-3 minutes, or until the eggs are set and cooked through.
7. Season and Garnish: Season the Bacalhau à Brás with salt and pepper to taste. Sprinkle chopped fresh parsley over the top for garnish.

8. Serve: Transfer the Bacalhau à Brás to a serving platter or individual plates. Garnish with black olives if desired. Serve hot and enjoy!

Bacalhau à Brás is often served as a main dish, accompanied by a fresh salad or steamed vegetables. It's a hearty and satisfying meal that's perfect for sharing with family and friends. Enjoy the rich flavors of this classic Portuguese dish!

Scottish Haggis

Ingredients:

- 1 sheep's pluck (heart, liver, and lungs), cleaned and trimmed
- 1 onion, finely chopped
- 1 cup steel-cut oats or oatmeal
- 1/2 cup beef suet, finely chopped
- 1 teaspoon salt
- 1/2 teaspoon black pepper
- 1/2 teaspoon ground coriander
- 1/2 teaspoon ground nutmeg
- 1/4 teaspoon ground cloves
- 1/4 teaspoon ground allspice
- 1/4 teaspoon cayenne pepper (optional)
- Sheep's stomach (or synthetic casing) for stuffing

Instructions:

1. Rinse the sheep's pluck under cold water and remove any excess fat, gristle, or connective tissue. Place the cleaned pluck in a large pot, cover with water, and bring to a boil. Reduce the heat and simmer for 2-3 hours, or until the meat is tender and cooked through. Remove the pluck from the pot and allow it to cool.
2. Once cooled, finely chop the cooked pluck, including the heart, liver, and lungs. In a large mixing bowl, combine the chopped pluck with the finely chopped onion, steel-cut oats, beef suet, salt, black pepper, ground coriander, ground nutmeg, ground cloves, ground allspice, and cayenne pepper (if using). Mix well to combine all the ingredients evenly.
3. Prepare the sheep's stomach (or synthetic casing) by thoroughly rinsing it under cold water and soaking it in salted water for at least 30 minutes. Rinse again and turn it inside out to remove any excess salt.
4. Stuff the prepared haggis mixture into the sheep's stomach (or synthetic casing), filling it about two-thirds full to allow room for expansion during cooking. Use kitchen twine to tie off the ends securely, leaving some space for the haggis to expand.
5. Place the stuffed haggis in a large pot and cover with water. Bring the water to a boil, then reduce the heat and simmer gently for 3-4 hours, or until the haggis is cooked through and firm to the touch.

6. Once cooked, carefully remove the haggis from the pot and let it rest for a few minutes before slicing and serving.

Traditionally, haggis is served with neeps (mashed turnips or swedes) and tatties (mashed potatoes), along with a drizzle of whisky sauce or gravy. It's often enjoyed as the main course during Burns Suppers, where it's accompanied by recitations of Robert Burns' poetry and songs.

While preparing haggis at home may seem daunting, many butchers and specialty stores offer pre-made haggis for purchase, making it more accessible to enjoy this iconic Scottish dish.

Swedish Meatballs

Ingredients:

For the meatballs:

- 1 lb (450g) ground beef
- 1/2 lb (225g) ground pork
- 1/2 cup breadcrumbs
- 1/4 cup milk
- 1 small onion, finely chopped
- 1 garlic clove, minced
- 1 egg
- 1 teaspoon salt
- 1/2 teaspoon black pepper
- 1/4 teaspoon ground allspice
- 1/4 teaspoon ground nutmeg
- 2 tablespoons unsalted butter, for frying

For the gravy:

- 2 tablespoons unsalted butter
- 2 tablespoons all-purpose flour
- 2 cups beef broth
- 1/2 cup heavy cream
- Salt and pepper to taste
- Lingonberry sauce, for serving
- Fresh parsley, chopped, for garnish (optional)

Instructions:

1. Prepare the Meatball Mixture: In a large mixing bowl, combine the ground beef, ground pork, breadcrumbs, milk, chopped onion, minced garlic, egg, salt, pepper, allspice, and nutmeg. Use your hands or a wooden spoon to mix everything together until well combined.

2. **Form the Meatballs:** Roll the meat mixture into small balls, about 1 inch in diameter. Place the formed meatballs on a baking sheet lined with parchment paper.
3. **Cook the Meatballs:** In a large skillet or frying pan, melt 2 tablespoons of butter over medium heat. Add the meatballs in batches, making sure not to overcrowd the pan. Cook the meatballs for about 8-10 minutes, turning them occasionally, until they are browned on all sides and cooked through. Transfer the cooked meatballs to a plate and cover them to keep warm.
4. **Make the Gravy:** In the same skillet used to cook the meatballs, melt 2 tablespoons of butter over medium heat. Sprinkle the flour over the melted butter and whisk continuously to make a roux. Cook the roux for 1-2 minutes until it turns golden brown.
5. **Add Broth and Cream:** Gradually pour the beef broth into the skillet, whisking constantly to prevent lumps from forming. Bring the mixture to a simmer and cook for 2-3 minutes until the gravy thickens slightly. Stir in the heavy cream and continue to simmer for another 2-3 minutes until the gravy reaches your desired consistency. Season with salt and pepper to taste.
6. **Serve:** Return the cooked meatballs to the skillet with the gravy, tossing gently to coat them in the sauce. Serve the Swedish meatballs hot, accompanied by lingonberry sauce on the side. Garnish with chopped fresh parsley if desired.
7. **Enjoy:** Enjoy these flavorful Swedish meatballs as a main course, served with mashed potatoes, egg noodles, or crusty bread. They're perfect for a cozy dinner or special occasion.

Swedish meatballs are a beloved comfort food that's easy to make at home. With their tender texture and rich gravy, they're sure to be a hit with family and friends alike!

Thai Tom Yum Goong (Spicy Shrimp Soup)

Ingredients:

- 10 cups water or chicken broth
- 1 lb (450g) large shrimp, peeled and deveined
- 6-8 kaffir lime leaves
- 2 stalks lemongrass, cut into 2-inch pieces and bruised
- 3-4 slices galangal (Thai ginger)
- 3-4 Thai bird's eye chilies, bruised (adjust to taste)
- 1 medium tomato, cut into wedges
- 1 small onion, sliced
- 1 cup mushrooms (straw mushrooms, button mushrooms, or shiitake mushrooms), sliced
- 2 tablespoons fish sauce
- 2 tablespoons lime juice
- 1 tablespoon sugar
- Salt to taste
- Fresh cilantro leaves for garnish
- Thai chili flakes or chopped fresh chili for extra heat (optional)

Instructions:

1. Prepare the Broth: In a large pot, bring the water or chicken broth to a boil over medium-high heat. Add the kaffir lime leaves, lemongrass, galangal slices, and bruised Thai bird's eye chilies. Let the broth simmer for about 5-10 minutes to infuse the flavors.
2. Add Vegetables and Shrimp: Add the tomato wedges, sliced onion, and mushrooms to the pot. Let them simmer in the broth for another 5 minutes until they start to soften. Then, add the peeled and deveined shrimp to the pot and cook for 2-3 minutes until they turn pink and opaque.
3. Season the Soup: Stir in the fish sauce, lime juice, and sugar to the pot. Taste the soup and adjust the seasoning with more fish sauce, lime juice, or sugar if needed. Season with salt to taste.
4. Garnish and Serve: Remove the pot from the heat. Ladle the Tom Yum Goong into serving bowls, making sure to distribute the shrimp, vegetables, and aromatics evenly. Garnish each bowl with fresh cilantro leaves and Thai chili flakes or chopped fresh chili for extra heat if desired.

5. Enjoy: Serve the Tom Yum Goong hot as a starter or main dish, accompanied by steamed rice or Thai noodles. Enjoy the bold and tangy flavors of this classic Thai soup!

Tom Yum Goong is a versatile dish that can be customized according to your taste preferences. You can adjust the level of spiciness by adding more or fewer chili peppers, and you can also add other ingredients such as tofu, seafood, or chicken to make it even heartier. Experiment with different combinations of ingredients to create your perfect bowl of Tom Yum Goong!

Tunisian Couscous

Ingredients:

For the Couscous:

- 2 cups couscous
- 2 cups water or vegetable broth
- 1 tablespoon olive oil
- Salt to taste

For the Stew:

- 1 lb (450g) lamb or chicken, cut into chunks
- 2 tablespoons olive oil
- 1 onion, finely chopped
- 2 cloves garlic, minced
- 2 carrots, peeled and diced
- 2 zucchinis, diced
- 1 bell pepper, diced
- 1 can (14 oz) chickpeas, drained and rinsed
- 2 tomatoes, diced
- 2 tablespoons tomato paste
- 1 teaspoon ground cumin
- 1 teaspoon ground coriander
- 1 teaspoon paprika
- 1/2 teaspoon ground cinnamon
- Salt and pepper to taste
- Fresh cilantro or parsley, chopped, for garnish
- Lemon wedges, for serving

Instructions:

1. Prepare the Couscous: Place the couscous in a large bowl. In a separate saucepan, bring the water or vegetable broth to a boil. Stir in the olive oil and salt. Pour the boiling liquid over the couscous, cover the bowl with a lid or plastic

wrap, and let it sit for about 5-10 minutes, or until the couscous absorbs the liquid and becomes fluffy. Fluff the couscous with a fork to separate the grains.
2. Prepare the Stew: In a large pot or Dutch oven, heat the olive oil over medium heat. Add the chopped onion and minced garlic, and sauté until softened and fragrant, about 2-3 minutes.
3. Brown the Meat: Add the chunks of lamb or chicken to the pot, and cook until browned on all sides, about 5-7 minutes.
4. Add Vegetables and Spices: Stir in the diced carrots, zucchinis, bell pepper, chickpeas, diced tomatoes, and tomato paste. Add the ground cumin, ground coriander, paprika, ground cinnamon, salt, and pepper. Mix everything together until well combined.
5. Simmer the Stew: Pour enough water into the pot to cover the ingredients, about 2-3 cups. Bring the mixture to a simmer, then reduce the heat to low. Cover the pot and let the stew simmer gently for about 30-40 minutes, or until the meat is tender and the vegetables are cooked through. Stir occasionally, and add more water if needed to prevent the stew from drying out.
6. Serve: To serve, spoon the fluffy couscous onto serving plates or bowls. Ladle the stew over the couscous. Garnish with chopped fresh cilantro or parsley, and serve with lemon wedges on the side for squeezing over the couscous.

Tunisian couscous is a hearty and comforting dish that's perfect for sharing with family and friends. Enjoy the rich flavors and aromatic spices of this traditional Tunisian meal!

Ukrainian Varenyky (Pierogi)

Ingredients:

For the dough:

- 2 cups all-purpose flour
- 1 large egg
- 1/2 cup water
- 1/4 teaspoon salt

For the filling:

- 2 cups mashed potatoes (cooled)
- 1 medium onion (finely chopped and sautéed until golden)
- Salt and pepper to taste
- Optional: grated cheese, cooked ground meat, sauerkraut

For serving:

- Sour cream
- Chopped fresh dill (optional)
- Butter (optional)

Instructions:

1. Prepare the dough:
    - In a mixing bowl, combine the flour and salt.
    - Make a well in the center and add the egg and water.
    - Gradually mix the wet ingredients into the flour until a dough forms.
    - Knead the dough on a lightly floured surface until smooth.
    - Cover the dough with a damp towel and let it rest for about 30 minutes.
2. Make the filling:
    - If using mashed potatoes, mix them with the sautéed onions, salt, and pepper. You can also add cheese, cooked ground meat, or sauerkraut to the filling if desired.
3. Form the dumplings:

- Roll out the dough on a floured surface to about 1/8 inch thickness.
- Using a round cutter or a glass, cut out circles from the dough.
- Place a small spoonful of filling in the center of each circle.
- Fold the dough over the filling to form a half-moon shape.
- Press the edges together firmly to seal, either by crimping with a fork or by pinching the edges together.

4. Cook the Varenyky:
    - Bring a large pot of salted water to a boil.
    - Carefully drop the Varenyky into the boiling water, a few at a time, to avoid overcrowding.
    - Cook for about 3-4 minutes, or until they float to the surface and are cooked through.
    - Remove the cooked Varenyky with a slotted spoon and transfer them to a serving dish.

5. Serve:
    - Serve the Varenyky hot with sour cream on the side.
    - Optionally, garnish with chopped fresh dill and a drizzle of melted butter.

Enjoy your homemade Ukrainian Varenyky!

Venezuelan Arepas

Ingredients:

- 2 cups pre-cooked cornmeal (such as Harina P.A.N.)
- 1 1/2 to 2 cups warm water
- 1 teaspoon salt
- 1 tablespoon vegetable oil (optional, for greasing the pan)

Instructions:

1. Mix the dough:
   - In a large mixing bowl, combine the pre-cooked cornmeal and salt.
   - Gradually add the warm water, mixing with your hands until a soft, smooth dough forms. The dough should hold together and not be too dry or too wet.
   - Knead the dough for a few minutes until it becomes elastic. Let it rest for about 5 minutes.
2. Shape the arepas:
   - Divide the dough into equal portions and roll each portion into a ball.
   - Flatten each ball to form a disk, about 1/2 to 3/4 inch thick. You can shape them into rounds or slightly flattened spheres, depending on your preference.
3. Cook the arepas:
   - Preheat a non-stick skillet or griddle over medium heat. If using, add a small amount of vegetable oil to lightly grease the surface.
   - Carefully place the shaped arepas on the skillet or griddle, making sure not to overcrowd them.
   - Cook for about 5-7 minutes on each side, or until golden brown and crispy on the outside. You may need to adjust the heat to prevent burning.
4. Finish cooking:
   - Once both sides are golden brown, transfer the arepas to a baking sheet.
   - Finish cooking them in a preheated oven at 350°F (175°C) for about 15-20 minutes, or until they sound hollow when tapped on the bottom.
5. Serve:
   - Let the arepas cool slightly before slicing them open horizontally, like a sandwich.
   - Fill them with your favorite ingredients such as shredded beef, chicken, black beans, avocado, cheese, or any other desired fillings.
   - Enjoy your Venezuelan arepas warm and freshly filled!

Arepas are incredibly versatile and can be enjoyed with a wide variety of fillings, so feel free to get creative with your combinations!

Welsh Rarebit

Ingredients:

- 2 tablespoons unsalted butter
- 2 tablespoons all-purpose flour
- 1 cup milk
- 2 cups grated sharp cheddar cheese
- 1 tablespoon Worcestershire sauce
- 1 teaspoon Dijon mustard
- Salt and pepper to taste
- 4-6 slices of bread (traditionally toasted sourdough or a similar hearty bread)

Optional additions for extra flavor:

- A pinch of cayenne pepper or paprika
- A splash of beer or ale
- Chopped fresh herbs such as thyme or parsley

Instructions:

1. Prepare the cheese sauce:
    - In a medium saucepan, melt the butter over medium heat.
    - Stir in the flour to form a paste (roux) and cook for 1-2 minutes, stirring constantly.
    - Gradually whisk in the milk, stirring constantly to prevent lumps from forming.
    - Cook the mixture until it thickens and begins to bubble, about 3-5 minutes.
    - Reduce the heat to low and gradually stir in the grated cheese until it melts and the sauce is smooth.
    - Stir in the Worcestershire sauce, Dijon mustard, salt, and pepper. Taste and adjust seasoning as needed.
    - If using optional additions like cayenne pepper or beer, add them at this point and stir until well incorporated.
2. Toast the bread:
    - Toast the slices of bread until golden brown and crispy. You can do this in a toaster, under the broiler, or in a skillet.
3. Assemble and serve:

- Arrange the toasted bread slices on a baking sheet or oven-safe dish.
- Generously spoon the cheese sauce over the toast, covering each slice completely.
- If desired, sprinkle additional grated cheese on top for extra cheesiness.
- Place the Welsh Rarebit under a preheated broiler for 2-3 minutes, or until the cheese sauce is bubbly and lightly golden brown on top.
- Keep a close eye on it to prevent burning.
- Serve immediately, garnished with chopped fresh herbs if desired.

Welsh Rarebit makes for a comforting and satisfying meal or snack, perfect for any time of day!

Zimbabwean Sadza (Cornmeal Porridge)

Ingredients:

- 2 cups white maize meal (cornmeal)
- 4-5 cups water
- Salt (optional)

Instructions:

1. Prepare the water:
    - In a large pot, bring the water to a boil over medium-high heat.
2. Add the maize meal:
    - Once the water is boiling, gradually add the maize meal to the pot while stirring continuously with a wooden spoon or whisk. This helps to prevent lumps from forming.
3. Cook the sadza:
    - Reduce the heat to medium-low and continue to stir the mixture until it thickens and begins to bubble.
    - At this point, cover the pot with a lid and let the sadza simmer for about 15-20 minutes, stirring occasionally to prevent sticking.
4. Adjust consistency and seasoning:
    - If the sadza becomes too thick during cooking, you can add more water, a little at a time, until you reach your desired consistency.
    - Optionally, add salt to taste, stirring well to distribute it evenly throughout the porridge.
5. Serve:
    - Once the sadza is cooked and reaches the desired consistency, remove it from the heat.
    - Allow it to rest for a few minutes before serving.
    - Traditionally, sadza is served in small mounds or portions on individual plates or bowls, alongside various relishes, stews, or sauces.

Sadza is typically enjoyed as a side dish, served alongside dishes like beef, chicken, vegetable stews, or sauces such as peanut butter or tomato-based gravies. It's a versatile and filling staple that forms the foundation of many Zimbabwean meals.

Afghan Kabuli Pulao

Ingredients:

For the rice:

- 2 cups basmati rice, rinsed and soaked in water for 30 minutes
- 1 large onion, thinly sliced
- 1/4 cup vegetable oil or ghee
- 4 cups water
- Salt to taste

For the meat:

- 1 lb (450g) lamb or beef, cut into cubes
- 1 large onion, finely chopped
- 3 cloves garlic, minced
- 1/2 teaspoon ground turmeric
- 1/2 teaspoon ground cardamom
- 1/2 teaspoon ground cinnamon
- 1/2 teaspoon ground black pepper
- Salt to taste
- 2 tablespoons vegetable oil or ghee
- 1/4 cup raisins (optional)
- 1/4 cup slivered almonds (optional)

For garnish:

- Chopped fresh cilantro or parsley
- Sliced carrots (fried until golden for garnish, optional)

Instructions:

1. Prepare the rice:
    - In a large pot, heat the vegetable oil or ghee over medium heat. Add the sliced onion and cook until golden brown and caramelized.

- Drain the soaked rice and add it to the pot with the caramelized onions. Stir well to coat the rice with the oil.
- Add the water and salt to taste. Bring to a boil, then reduce the heat to low, cover, and simmer for about 15-20 minutes, or until the rice is cooked and fluffy. Remove from heat and set aside.

2. Prepare the meat:
    - In a separate large skillet or pot, heat the vegetable oil or ghee over medium-high heat.
    - Add the chopped onion and sauté until soft and translucent.
    - Add the minced garlic and cook for another minute until fragrant.
    - Add the cubed meat to the skillet and brown on all sides.
    - Sprinkle the turmeric, cardamom, cinnamon, black pepper, and salt over the meat. Stir well to coat the meat with the spices.
    - Pour in enough water to cover the meat, then reduce the heat to low, cover, and simmer for about 1 to 1.5 hours, or until the meat is tender and cooked through. Add more water if necessary to prevent it from drying out.
    - If using, add the raisins and slivered almonds to the meat during the last 10-15 minutes of cooking.

3. Assemble the Kabuli Pulao:
    - Once the meat and rice are ready, transfer the cooked rice to a large serving platter or dish.
    - Arrange the cooked meat on top of the rice.
    - Garnish with chopped fresh cilantro or parsley.
    - Optionally, garnish with fried sliced carrots for added flavor and presentation.

4. Serve:
    - Serve the Kabuli Pulao hot, with additional garnishes if desired.
    - Enjoy this delicious and aromatic Afghan dish with family and friends!

Kabuli Pulao is often served with yogurt or a simple salad on the side. It's a hearty and flavorful meal that's sure to impress!

www.ingramcontent.com/pod-product-compliance
Lightning Source LLC
LaVergne TN
LVHW061942070526
838199LV00060B/3932